Understanding and Teaching the Indirect Object in Spanish

Understanding and Teaching the Indirect Object in Spanish presents an easy-to-understand approach to all aspects of direct and indirect objects in Spanish. Distinguishing between direct and indirect objects can pose challenges for learners and is almost impossible to do using the tools that linguists have traditionally used. This book offers two simple, all-encompassing inferences that allow learners to tackle this area of language by intuitively inferring the distinction, as native speakers do, between verber and verbed.

This book will be of interest to teachers and learners of Spanish and other second languages, as well as linguists interested in argument structure, second language acquisition, second language teaching or pedagogy, and multilingualism.

Luis H. González is Professor of Spanish and Linguistics at Wake Forest University, United States. He completed his Ph.D. at the University of California, Davis. His main areas of research are semantic roles, case, reflexivization, clitic doubling, differential object marking, dichotomies in languages, Spanish linguistics, and second language learning. He has written and co-authored six successful titles on these topics.

Verber, Verbed Grammar Series
Series Author: Luis H. González, *Wake Forest University, USA*

Cómo entender y cómo enseñar por y para
Luis H. González

Four Dichotomies in Spanish
Adjective Position, Adjectival Clauses, Ser/Estar, and Preterite/Imperfect
Luis H. González

The Fundamentally Simple Logic of Language
Learning a Second Language with the Tools of the Native Speaker
Luis H. González

Understanding and Teaching Reflexive Sentences in Spanish
Luis H. González

Understanding and Teaching the Indirect Object in Spanish
Luis H. González

For more information about this series, please visit: www.routledge.com/Verber-Verbed-Grammar/book-series/VVG

Understanding and Teaching the Indirect Object in Spanish

Luis H. González

Spanish List Advisor
Javier Muñoz-Basols

LONDON AND NEW YORK

First published 2024
by Routledge
4 Park Square, Milton Park, Abingdon, Oxon OX14 4RN

and by Routledge
605 Third Avenue, New York, NY 10158

Routledge is an imprint of the Taylor & Francis Group, an informa business

© 2024 Luis H. González

The right of Luis H. González to be identified as author of this work has been asserted in accordance with sections 77 and 78 of the Copyright, Designs and Patents Act 1988.

All rights reserved. No part of this book may be reprinted or reproduced or utilised in any form or by any electronic, mechanical, or other means, now known or hereafter invented, including photocopying and recording, or in any information storage or retrieval system, without permission in writing from the publishers.

Trademark notice: Product or corporate names may be trademarks or registered trademarks, and are used only for identification and explanation without intent to infringe.

British Library Cataloguing-in-Publication Data
A catalogue record for this book is available from the British Library

Library of Congress Cataloging-in-Publication Data
Names: González, Luis, 1957– author.
Title: Understanding and teaching the indirect object in Spanish / Luis H. González.
Description: Abingdon, Oxon ; New York, NY : Routledge, 2024. | Series: Verber, verbed grammar | Includes bibliographical references and index.
Identifiers: LCCN 2023014462 (print) | LCCN 2023014463 (ebook)
Subjects: LCSH: Spanish language—Indirect object. | Spanish language—Direct object. | Spanish language—Verb phrase. | Spanish language—Study and teaching—Foreign speakers.
Classification: LCC PC4369 .G63 2024 (print) | LCC PC4369 (ebook) | DDC 465—dc23/eng/20230605
LC record available at https://lccn.loc.gov/2023014462
LC ebook record available at https://lccn.loc.gov/2023014463

ISBN: 978-1-032-51293-8 (hbk)
ISBN: 978-1-032-51939-5 (pbk)
ISBN: 978-1-003-40452-1 (ebk)

DOI: 10.4324/9781003404521

Typeset in Times New Roman
by Apex CoVantage, LLC

To those who have dreams that they have not achieved yet. You never lose hope. Never!

This dedication was inspired by a college student battling an unknown neurological disorder. Your family and friends are rooting for you, MB!

Contents

List of tables x
Acknowledgements xi

1 **Subject and direct object or <u>verber</u> and verbed?** 1

   1.1 *Native speakers are computing <u>verber</u> and verbed, not subject and direct object* 1
   1.2 *How* verbed *reveals a difference that* subject *hides* 1
   1.3 *Sentences with three participants* 3
   1.4 <u>*Verbees*</u> *in Spanish (and other languages) that are not expressed as verbees in English* 4
   Notes 6
   References 7

2 **Distinguishing some direct objects from an indirect object can be a puzzle; distinguishing a verbed from a <u>verbee</u> is an inference that always works** 8

   2.1 *Introduction* 8
   2.2 *Distinguishing some direct objects from an indirect object can be a puzzle; distinguishing a **verbed** from a <u>verbee</u> is an inference that always works* 9
   2.3 *False verbees, true verbees, dialectal* leísmo, *and general* leísmo: *everything is connected* 12
   2.4 *In the classroom* 21
   2.5 *Conclusions* 24
   2.6 *Exercises* 25
   Notes 31
   References 33

3   **Against the need for 11 or more types of sentences with an indirect object in Spanish and in other languages**   37

   3.1 Eleven types of sentences with a dative (an indirect object) in Spanish 37
   3.2 The <u>verbee</u> in three-participant sentences and in two-participant sentences 41
      3.2.1 Sentences with <u>verber</u>, **verbed**, and <u>verbee</u> 41
      3.2.2 Sentences with <u>verber</u>, **[verbed]**, and <u>verbee</u> 41
      3.2.3 Sentences with <u>verbee</u> and **verbed** (verberless sentences) 43
   3.3 Types of sentences with a dative (an indirect object) in four other languages 46
      3.3.1 Types of sentences with an indirect object in Latin (Van Hoecke 1996: 3–37) 46
      3.3.2 Types of sentences with an indirect object in Portuguese (de Andrade Berlinck 1996: 119–151) 48
      3.3.3 Types of datives with an indirect object in French (Melis 1996: 40–51). Three-term constructions 50
      3.3.4 Types of sentences with an indirect object in Polish (Rudzka-Ostyn 1996: 341–394) 54
   3.4 Connecting <u>verber</u>, **verbed**, and <u>verbee</u> in Polish, in Italian, and in other languages 56
   3.5 In the classroom 58
   3.6 Conclusions 59
   Notes 60
   References 63

4   **A pronoun does not double its indirect object; the latter drops when it is known information in postverbal position**   65

   4.1 Does a pronoun "double" its indirect object or does the indirect object drop when it is known information? 65
   4.2 Indirect object pronoun doubling turned upside down 68
   4.3 Is accusative a *(personal* a*)* the same as the a that introduces an indirect object? 73

4.4 Postverbal _verbee_ drop (when known information/
world knowledge) encompasses several rules of
indirect object pronoun "doubling" 75
    4.4.1 Three rules of indirect object doubling with
         a pronoun in Gutiérrez Ordóñez (1999) 78
    4.4.2 Rules of _indirect object_ (and direct object)
         pronoun doubling in RAE/ASALE (2010) 83
    4.4.3 Other rules of indirect object pronoun
         "doubling" 91
4.5 Some evidence against the distinction between
argumental and non argumental indirect objects 92
4.6 _Verbee_ drop in the classroom 94
4.7 Conclusions 95
4.8 Exercises (answers provided) 97
Notes 104
References 107

Index 110

Tables

1.1	Sample of <u>verbees</u> (IOs) in Spanish that are not expressed as verbees in English	6
2.1	*Incomodar* has <u>verber</u> and **verbed**; *importar* has **verbed** and <u>verbee</u>	10
2.2	Translation of Table 2.1 into English	10
2.3	*Molestar, sorprender, preocupar, acusar, maltratar, and golpear* pronominalized with an IO pronoun (*les*) and with a DO pronoun (*las*)	13
2.4	*Preocupar* 'worry' with an IO pronoun (*le/les*) and with a DO pronoun (*la/las, lo/los*).	14
2.5	The difference between true <u>verbees</u> and false verbees (**verbeds**)	17
2.6	How "**a Margarita**" (**verbed**) is different from "a Margarita" (<u>verbee</u>)	20
2.7	*Incomodar* has <u>verber</u>, **verbed**; *importar* has <u>verbee</u>, **verbed**	23
3.1	Types of sentences with an indirect object in Spanish. MC Cuervo's examples 29–39 (Cuervo 2003: 29–30)	38
3.2	Types of sentences with an indirect object in Latin	47
3.3	Types of sentences with an indirect object in Portuguese	49
3.4	Types of sentences with an indirect object in French. Three-term constructions	51
3.5	Types of sentences with an indirect object in French (Melis 1996: 51–57). Two-term constructions	53
3.6	Types of sentences with an indirect object in French (Melis 1996: 57–59). Extensions of the attributive dative	54
3.7	Types of sentences with an indirect object in Polish	55
4.1	Frequency of indirect object pronoun alone, indirect object pronoun + indirect object, and indirect object alone (Vázquez Rozas 2006: 84)	71
4.2	Indirect object pronoun alone (clitic), indirect object doubling (cl doubling), and indirect object (NP) alone (Belloro 2007: 141)	71
4.3	Frequency of the forms of the indirect object (Weissenrieder 1995: 173)	71

Acknowledgements

Teaching is finite. Learning is infinite. So is love. The love for learning is also infinite. And it can very easily become an obsession. One of my students told me four years ago, "Professor, you do not like grammar. You are *obsessed* with grammar". She is correct. She was one of my students, although she never took a class with me – she did an independent study with me, though. Her name is Savarni Sanka, and she earned a Rhodes Scholarship in 2020. I loved her comment, which was one of many laughs we shared. I have quoted her comment dozens of times. I remember sharing her observation with Dr. Antonio Fábregas, a famous linguist, who added, "We have to be obsessed in the type of work we do".

One day, Sav asked me what restrictive and non-restrictive relative clauses were. I replied, "I am going to experiment on you. I am going to explain that concept to you orally, without a piece of paper". I did. She understood the concept. That indicates how far an explanation on the right track can go. That was enough for her to start processing restrictiveness and non-restrictiveness when reading and writing. She wrote an excellent paper on adjective position in which she used novel examples coming from her personal experience. The concept of (non) restrictiveness is the same in adjective position and in relative (adjectival) clauses.

An infinite love for learning is what brings scholars to research a topic such as the indirect object. I say the **indirect object** in the singular because it has one *unified* meaning, as speakers (and linguists) would like it. I would like to recognize here many scholars who came before me and explored some of the issues explored in this book. Some of those scholars are quoted with all due respect, even when I had to write that their proposal should be re-thought. *Improved* is perhaps a better word. That is part of the scientific pursuit. Other scholars did not get quoted because there is a great deal of selecting and limiting in writing. The discussion of each point must have an order and a flow that says enough that is relevant but is not overwhelming. There are tangents that can derail a scholar literally at every sentence. I have gotten that warning several times from reviewers of my scholarship. The trick is a word that is "a classic" in many aspects of life: balance. The writer tries to anticipate the questions that readers might have. At every sentence. Without getting off on unnecessary tangents. An insightful undergraduate student (and now a physician), Saloni Patolia, once asked me, "How does a professor decide what goes into a textbook?" I did not have a good answer at the time. I promised her that I would be thinking about her question. Now I can answer that question with one word: relevance. Is it relevant for a college class that meets 50 minutes three times a week for 15 or so weeks? Is it a good use of the time of 15 to 30 students in a (language) class? In this case, does it highlight the most relevant and hopefully transformative information on the indirect object?

There are tens, perhaps hundreds of dissertations and master theses on the indirect object in each of several languages. Conceivably in many languages. There are hundreds, perhaps thousands of articles written on the indirect object in many languages. There are probably at least one hundred books on the indirect object in all languages combined. I write these observations here to highlight that there are many more scholars who could not be quoted than the few whose work I ended up mentioning. A heartfelt thanks to all of them. I would like to mention a few scholars who did not make it to the references, but whose research is directly connected with objects or pronouns: F. Ackerman, Raúl Aranovich, M. Baker, J. Bresnan, P. Farrell, Ch. Fillmore, J. Gruber, R. Hudson, R. Jackendoff, L. King, J. Lidz, J. Ormazábal, J. Moore, D. Perlmutter, J. Romero, I. Sag, A. Zwicky. Stan Whitley and Robert D. van Valin, Jr. get an explicit mention because both of them were my teachers. Whitley, formally and informally. Van Valin, informally. I just sat in two of his classes at the University of California at Davis, California. I learned argumentation in syntax with both of them, among many other lessons. Their classes were places where learners experienced thinking happening. I still remember some beautifully magic moments in those classes!

Most of the writing and all of the final reviewing of this book were done during the summer and fall of 2022, thanks to a sabbatical leave from Wake Forest University. Thank you to all involved! Several colleagues or friends answered a few questions on languages they know. Jessie Craft, Hosun Kim, Jeff Lerner, Sol Miguel-Prendes, Stephanie Pellet, Boston Woolfolk, and Silvia Tiboni-Craft are among the ones I remember now. Parts of this research were presented at the Slinki/Slise conference over several years. Audrey Dyer and Emily McCown, two undergraduate students at Wake Forest University, read each chapter and gave me detailed feedback. Mary Friedman, a dear colleague and friend, also read the whole manuscript and provided priceless feedback. ¡Muchísimas gracias de todo corazón a todas y a todos! Thanks a lot also to Samantha Vale-Noya, Tassia Watson, and their Routledge team on the other side of the world and on the other side of this research program. Their team includes three anonymous reviewers who provided valuable feedback that significantly improved the original manuscript. Thanks, finally, to my wife and children for their patience. They finally see now how all this work is going somewhere.

Luis H. González
Winston-Salem, NC, January 2023

1 Subject and direct object or verber and verbed?

1.1 Native speakers are computing verber and verbed, not subject and direct object[1]

González (2021) provides ample evidence that children understand and use SUBJECT and DIRECT OBJECT in any sentence not because they have learned or have an implicit knowledge of these two grammatical relations.[2] In a sentence like (1) below, *Ángela* is expressed as the subject and *a letter* as the direct object (DO) because speakers are intuitively and implicitly computing two simple entailments: a VERBER ENTAILMENT and a **VERBED** ENTAILMENT. If (1a) is true, then, which of the sentences in (1b-e) are true?

(1) a. Ángela sent **a letter**.
    b. Ángela was the sender.   (THE VERBER ENTAILMENT)
    c. #Ángela was the sent.[3]
    d. #**A letter** was the sender.
    e. **A letter** was (the) sent.   (THE **VERBED** ENTAILMENT)

If (1a) is true, the sentences in (1b,e) are also true. The sentence in (1b) is the VERBER ENTAILMENT; the one in (2e) is the **VERBED** ENTAILMENT. They are logical entailments that follow necessarily if (1a) is true. Of course, (1c,d) are not true if (1a) is true.

With the verber and **verbed** entailments, we understand why speakers of any language will say the equivalent of *Linguists propose the coolest theories all the time* and why no speaker says in any language the equivalent of **The coolest theories propose linguists all the time.*[4] The following section shows that verber and **verbed** are not just a different label for subject and direct object.

1.2 How *verbed* reveals a difference that *subject* hides

Let us now consider two sentences with just one participant. This participant is always the subject. We will see, however, that the subject can be the verber or the **verbed**:

DOI: 10.4324/9781003404521-1

2 Subject and direct object or <u>verber</u> and **verbed**?

(2) a. <u>Ángela</u> studied.
  b. **Taxes** were increased.
  c. **Taxes** increased.

Let us apply the <u>verber</u> entailment and the **verbed** entailment to these sentences:

(3) a. <u>Ángela</u> is the studier (i.e. the student).
  b. #Ángela is the studied.
  c. #Taxes were the increaser.
  d. **Taxes** were (the) increased.

It turns out that (3a) and (3d) are entailments from (2a-c). Those entailments show that the subject of (2a) is *Ángela* and she is the "<u>studier</u>" (student). They also show that **taxes** are the **increased**. Since the only participant in an intransitive sentence is the subject, observe that the subject of (2b,c) is the **increased**, not the <u>increaser</u>. Thus, the <u>VERBER</u> ENTAILMENT and the **VERBED** ENTAILMENT show that the subject of a sentence can be the <u>verber</u> or the **verbed**.

Sentences (2a-c) are INTRANSITIVE because they have just one participant. It seems more appropriate to call sentences (2b,c) INTRANSITIVIZED than intransitive. These two sentences are a syntactic variation of the transitive sentence *<u>the government</u> increased **taxes***. The latter is the underlying sentence called the active voice sentence. Sentence (2b) is the passive voice alternation. We will call sentences like (2b,c) intransitivized sentences from now on.

TRANSITIVE: a sentence is transitive if it has a <u>verber</u> and a **verbed** (González 2021: 6).

INTRANSITIVE: a sentence is intransitive (or INTRANSITIVIZED) if it has either a <u>verber</u> or a **verbed**, but not both.

Now we are ready to propose that native speakers determine who/what is the subject and who/what is the DO in a sentence by applying the following rule (González 2021: 6):

(4) <u>Verber</u> and **Verbed** Argument Selection Principle (VVASP):[5]

  The participant in a sentence that passes the <u>verber</u> entailment is expressed as the subject; the participant that passes the **verbed** entailment is expressed as the direct object of a transitive sentence, but as the subject of a sentence without a <u>verber</u>.

ARGUMENT is the specialized term in linguistics and philosophy for the "core" participants in a sentence. In terms of this book, <u>verber</u>, **verbed**, and verbee are the traditional arguments. Other participants are ADJUNTS. Arguments are presumably "selected" by the verb. Adjuncts are more freely added or deleted. Roughly speaking, adjuncts are called *complementos circunstanciales* 'circumstantial complements' in traditional Spanish grammar.

Up to this point, we have seen what transitive, intransitive, and intransitivized sentences are. A transitive sentence has a verber and a **verbed**; an intransitive sentence has a verber or a **verbed**, but not both; an intransitivized sentence is a sentence from which either its verber or its **verbed** was omitted. An important point of understanding grammar with verber and **verbed** is that the subject of an intransitive (or an intransitivized) sentence can be the verber or the **verbed**, a distinction that the notion of subject has blurred for over 21 centuries. For example, the subject of all sentences in the passive voice is a **verbed**. The subject of UNACCUSATIVE verbs (*appear, belong, cost, happen, matter, occur, remain, seem*, etc.) is the **verbed**. See González (2021, Chapter 5), for a discussion of the true *gustar* verbs in Spanish (the equivalent in Spanish of verbs like *belong, happen*, etc.). As González (2022, Chapter 2) shows, the subject of sentences with a "reflexive" pronoun is the **verbed** or the verbee.

UNACCUSATIVE verbs are verbs whose only object must be an indirect object (IO), like *gustar* 'like', *pertenecer* 'belong', *ocurrir* 'happen/occur', etc. UNACCUSATIVE verbs are VERBERLESS, but not subjectless. In the absence of a verber in a sentence, the **verbed** (or the verbee) is "promoted" to subject position. See González (2021, Chapters 4 and 5).

1.3 Sentences with three participants

Consider now sentence (5) in English:

(5) We sent Grandma **our children**.

It is uncontroversial who the sender is (*we*). Is it clear who the **sent** is? Is *Grandma* the sent or are *our children* the sent? Sentences (6a,b) will help readers who are not sure. The sentence in (5) is synonymous only with one of them:

(6) a. We sent **our children** to Grandma.
 b. #We sent Grandma to our children.

Sentences (5) and (6a) are synonymous. The **sent** in (5) and in (6a) are *our children*. Then, who or what is *Grandma*? *Grandma* is the beneficiary (the recipient) in an event of sending someone to her. *Grandma* is the beneficiary not only in (6a) but also in (5).

As González (2021: 11) shows, the indirect object (IO) is the participant who benefits or suffers some harm as a result from the event expressed in a sentence. For this reason, the terms BENEFICIARY (or MALEFICIARY) are often used to refer to the referent of an IO. Gil (1982: 122) called the participant expressed as an IO of the equivalent in Hebrew of verbs like *belong, be born, matter, happen, seem* the benefactee or the maleface. A fitting generalization for benefactee and malefactee is VERBEE (see González 2021, Chapter 1). The reader is invited to determine verber, **verbed**, and verbee in the following sentences. Please do not proceed with the reading if you would like to do the exercise before reading the answers.

(7) a. We sent a beautiful bouquet of flowers to Grandma.
   b. We sent Grandma a beautiful bouquet of flowers.
   c. A beautiful bouquet of flowers was sent to Grandma (by us).
   d. Grandma was sent a beautiful bouquet of flowers.

It is uncontroversial that we is the sender; *a beautiful bouquet of flowers* is the sent, and Grandma is the benefactee (verbee), regardless of the fact that we can be the subject (7a,b), a "*by phrase*" (7c), or it can be left out altogether (7d). A *beautiful bouquet of flowers* can be the direct object (7a,d), the secondary object (7b), or the subject (7c). Grandma can be the IO (7a,c), the primary object (7b), or the subject (7d). Thus, in variations of the same sentence, as in (7a-d), verber, **verbed**, and verbee are CONSTANT and more easily identifiable than subject, DO, and IO, whereas subject, DO, and IO vary and are more difficult to identify, as Chapter 2 shows.

Let us now repeat sentences (7a,c,d) above as (8a-c) below to show readers a "corollary" that follows from the Verber/Verbed Argument Selection Principle in (4) above:

(8) a. We sent **a beautiful bouquet of flowers** to Grandma.
   b. **A beautiful bouquet of flowers** was sent to Grandma (by us).
   c. Grandma was sent **a beautiful bouquet of flowers**.[6]

(9) If there is a verber in a sentence, it is always the subject. If there is no verber, the **verbed** or the verbee is promoted to subject position.

1.4 Verbees in Spanish (and other languages) that are not expressed as verbees in English[7]

A graduate student who was a major of Spanish in her undergraduate studies told this author in 2021 that she never had a professor of Spanish call her attention about the indirect object in Spanish (Mackenzie Krol, PC 2021). She was as surprised about discovering the PRODUCTIVITY of IOs in Spanish as I was that IOs had never been called to her attention. A phenomenon is PRODUCTIVE if it is a frequent pattern in the language. The IO is a very frequent pattern in Spanish and in many other languages. Only the first two sentences of the 11 sentences with an IO discussed by MC Cuervo (2003: 29–39) are expressed with an indirect object in English. Chapter 3 discusses those 11 types of sentences. Many IOs in Spanish are expressed in English with a preposition + object (*at, away, in, from, on*, etc.) or with a possessive phrase.

Another important factor contributing to blurring the distinction between IOs and DOs in English is the DOUBLE OBJECT CONSTRUCTION (DOC).[8] The sentence *we sent Grandma* **our children** is the DOC variation of the sentence *we send* **our children** *to Grandma*. Bresnan & Nikitina (2010) refer to the first object in the DOC (*Grandma*) as a dative NP and to the dative in the second sentence as a dative PP (*to Grandma*). Bresnan & Nikitina (2010) also report that in a corpus they used for their study (*Switchboard*, a telephone speech corpus reported in Godfrey & Holliman & McDaniel 1992), 78.6% of datives were DOC. When only first and second person datives were counted, that percentage increased to 91%.

The following table (the version in Spanish from sentences from five different languages discussed in Chapter 3) shows different ways in which English expresses what is expressed with an IO in many languages. Many of those languages still maintain a distinction between IOs and DOs in their pronoun system (at least in the third person, as shown below for Spanish). English does not distinguish an IO from a DO (or from the object of a preposition) when that object is a pronoun (or replaced with a pronoun): *me, you, him, her, us, you* (plural)*, them*. Spanish, like many languages, distinguishes an IO from a DO only in the pronouns in the third person. *Me, te, LA/LO, nos, os, LAS/LOS* are the DO pronouns. *Me, te, LE, nos, os, LES* are the IO pronouns.

This book will have a few dozen exercises to practice verber, **verbed**, and verbee in Chapter 2 and Chapter 4.

The rest of this book shows that with the verber entailment and the **verbed** entailment, the understanding of sentences with an IO is simpler than descriptions of this phenomenon in textbooks and in scholarly work. Contra RAE/ASALE (2009: 2681), it is possible to unequivocally determine that the object in sentences like *es una lucha que le incomoda a muchos* 'it is a fight that makes many uncomfortable' is a DO, not an IO, as the sentences in Table 2.1 in Chapter 2 show. Chapter 3 shows that true IOs consistently indicate the participant who gets something, loses something, or to whom something belongs. With verber and **verbed**, there is no need to invoke different semantic roles (experiencer, goal, recipient, etc.) for the IO. Regular speakers understand sentences with an IO without knowing that the IO is presumably either a beneficiary, an experiencer, a goal, a possessor, or a recipient, etc. Therefore, it is not necessary to learn the 11 or so types of sentences with an IO, as in MC Cuervo (2003: 29–30) or as in RAE/ASALE (2010: 679–684), for example. Chapter 4 shows that an IO pronoun does not "double" its IO. Rather, the IO pronoun and the IO are part of the sentence, but the latter is dropped when it is known information or world knowledge.

6 *Subject and direct object or* verber *and* **verbed***?*

Table 1.1 Sample of verbees (IOs) in Spanish that are not expressed as verbees in English

The verbee is a true indirect object in Spanish	The participant is not a verbee. It is expressed with a preposition different from *to/for* in English
(Él) te deslizó **una palabra** al oído (a ti). El azul le va/viene/sienta/queda bien. ¡No le llegue tarde (a ella)! Paul le quitó **la bicicleta** a Andreína. Le compré **este reloj** (a él). (He = seller)	He dropped a word IN your ear. Blue goes well ON her. Do not arrive late ON her! Paul took away the bicycle FROM Andreína. I bought this watch FROM him.
A verbee in Spanish	English uses a possessive structure
La cabeza le da **vueltas**. **Una idea** le pasó por la cabeza (a él). La tintura le quemó **el pelo**. Alicia me limpió (lavó) **el abrigo**. A Carolina se le descompuso **el radio**. Pablo le admira **la paciencia** a Valeria. Le tiemblan **las manos**. Se me escaparon **varios errores de ortografía**.	HER/HIS head is spinning. An idea crossed HIS mind. The dye burned HIS hair. Alice cleaned MY coat. Carolina's radio broke. Pablo admires Valeria's patience. HER hands are trembling. (Something causes her hands to tremble.) Some spelling mistakes escaped MY attention.
A verbee in Spanish	English changed the verb from taking an IO to taking a DO or does not distinguish an IO from a DO (these people)
A Daniela no le gustan **los gatos**. A Laura le sobraron **20 dólares**. Eva le ayudó a esta gente. (Eva le dio ayuda a esta gente).	Daniela does not like cats. Laura had 20 dollars left. Eva helped these people. Eva gave help to these people.
False verbees in Spanish. See §2.3	True verbeds (DOs) in English as well
La fortuna favorece **al valiente**. (Already a false verbee in Latin. See §2.3.) El asunto le/lo preocupaba particularmente.	Fortune favors the brave. The issue concerned him quite particularly.

Notes

1 Sections 1.1 to 1.3 in this chapter are a slightly revised version of Chapter 1 in González (2022), reproduced here with permission from Taylor & Francis. It is a brief explanation of <u>VERBADORA/VERBADOR</u> 'VERBER', **VERBADA/VERBADO** 'VERBED', AND <u>VERBATARIA/VERBATARIO</u> 'VERBEE'.
2 Key terms will be capitalized when they are particularly relevant. They are explained in the same paragraph or in an endnote, as needed.
3 The notation "#" means that the sentence is not entailed by the sentence under discussion or is semantically anomalous. This notation comes from Huddleston & Pullum (2002: 35).

4 An asterisk (*) before a sentence means that native speakers rarely or never utter that sentence.
5 This argument selection principle is modelled after Dowty (1991: 576). See González (2021: 94–100).
6 Spanish does not allow passivization of an indirect object (*<u>la abuela</u> fue enviada **un hermoso ramo de flores**). The equivalent of this sentence is done with intransitivizing SE, the equivalent in Spanish of IO passivization (González 2022, Chapter 2):

A <u>la abuela</u> <u>se</u> <u>le</u> envió **un hermoso ramo de flores**. (= 8c)
'<u>Grandma</u> was sent **a beautiful bouquet of flowers**'.

7 Thanks to Mary Friedman, PC 2023, for suggesting that this explanation would help readers understand why Spanish uses the IO much more than English.
8 The DOC is part of the dative (IO) alternation/structure, one of the most researched structures in English. A search for "double object construction" in Google Scholar in March 2023 returned 9,030 results.

References

Bresnan, Joan & Nikitina, Tatiana. 2010. The gradience of the dative alternation. In Uyechi, Linda Ann & Wee, Lian Hee (eds.), *Reality exploration and discovery: Pattern interaction in language & life*, 161–184. Stanford, CA: CSLI. https://web.stanford.edu/group/cslipublications/cslipublications/site/9781575865881.shtml

Cuervo, María Cristina. 2003. Datives at large. Cambridge, MA: MIT Press. (Doctoral dissertation). www.ai.mit.edu/projects/dm/theses/cuervo03.pdf

Dowty, David. 1991. Thematic proto-roles and argument selection. *Language* 67. 547–619. www.jstor.org/stable/pdf/415037

Gil, David. 1982. Case marking, phonological size, and word order. *Syntax and semantics* 15. 117–141. www.worldcat.org/title/syntax-and-semantics-vol-15-studies-in-transitivity/oclc/924597895

Godfrey, John J. & Holliman, Edward C. & McDaniel, Jane. 1992. Switchboard: Telephone speech corpus for research and development. In *Proceedings of the International Conference on Acoustics, Speech, and Signal Processing* (ICASSP), 517–520. San Francisco, CA. https://ieeexplore.ieee.org/document/225858

González, Luis H. 2021. *The fundamentally simple logic of language: Learning a second language with the tools of the native speaker*. London: Routledge. www.routledge.com/9780367688318

González, Luis H. 2022. *Understanding and teaching reflexive sentences in Spanish*. London: Routledge. www.routledge.com/9781032101873

Huddleston, Rodney & Pullum, Geoffrey K. 2002. *The Cambridge grammar of the English language*. Cambridge: Cambridge University Press. https://doi.org/10.1017/9781316423530

RAE/ASALE (Real Academia Española y Asociación de Academias de la Lengua Española). 2009. *Nueva gramática de la lengua española. Sintaxis II*. Madrid: Espasa. www.rae.es/obras-academicas/gramatica/nueva-gramatica-morfologia-y-sintaxis

RAE/ASALE (Real Academia Española y Asociación de Academias de la Lengua Española). 2010. *Nueva gramática de la lengua española. Manual*. Bogotá: Editorial Planeta Colombiana S.A. www.rae.es/obras-academicas/gramatica/manual-de-la-nueva-gramatica

2 Distinguishing some direct objects from an indirect object can be a puzzle; distinguishing a verbed from a <u>verbee</u> is an inference that always works

2.1 Introduction

This chapter shows that some objects that look like an indirect object (IO) are really **verbeds** (direct objects).[1] The object in sentences with *aburrir* 'bore', *asustar* 'frighten', *impresionar* 'impress', *molestar* 'bother', *preocupar* 'worry', *sorprender* 'surprise', etc., is often TOPICALIZED, DUPLICATED, or replaced with an IO pronoun (*le/les*) instead of a direct object (DO) pronoun (*la/las/lo/los*).[2] That object is the **bored, frightened, impressed, bothered, worried, surprised**, and not really a <u>verbee</u>. Crucially, the subject of these verbs is the <u>borer, frightener, impressor, botherer, worrier, surpriser</u>. These verbs behave like *incomodar* 'make uncomfortable' in Table 2.1 below. They are used in transitive sentences; that is, sentences with a <u>verber</u> and a **verbed** (González 2021: 6). Interestingly, the **verbed**, by virtue of being ANIMATE (human, roughly speaking) looks like a <u>verbee</u>. On the other hand, verbs like *ocurrir* 'happen', *importar* 'matter', *pertenecer* 'belong', *quedar* 'remain', etc., are VERBERLESS. Since these verbs do not have a <u>verber</u>, the **verbed** moves to subject position (per the implication in 9 in Chapter 1), and the object of these verbs is a true <u>verbee</u>: a <u>benefactee</u> or a <u>malefactee</u>. Their subject is the ***happened, mattered, belonged, remained***, etc., and their object (more often than not animate) is a <u>happenee, matteree, belongee, remainee</u>, etc., who is mandatorily "doubled" with an IO pronoun, even when it is in postverbal position. If these verbs had a <u>verber</u>, speakers of English would say sentences like, *an accident happened me, *integrity matters me, *this computer belongs me, etc.[3] Tables 2.1 and 2.3 provide the evidence for the difference between verbs with <u>verber</u> and **verbed**, like *aburrir* 'bore' and those with **verbed** and <u>verbee</u>, like *pertenecer* 'belong to'.

2.2 Distinguishing some direct objects from an indirect object can be a puzzle; distinguishing a verbed from a <u>verbee</u> is an inference that always works

Consider the difficulty in telling apart DOs from IOs, as one can read in RAE/ASALE (2009: 2681). (Underlined in the original; bold added by this author):

> **No es posible**, saber, en efecto, si el segmento subrayado en el primero de los textos siguientes es objeto directo o indirecto, pero **no cabe duda de que es objeto indirecto** en el segundo:
>
>> [. . .] una alegría contagiosa, sardónica y malsana que incomodaba <u>**a Cristico**</u> y deleitaba a su madre (Herrera Luque, *Casa*); Es una lucha que quizá **le** incomode **a muchos**, pero es una lucha auténtica (Excélsior 1/9/2000).

Translation by this author:

> **It is not possible** to know, in fact, if the underlined segment in the first of the following texts is a DO or an IO, but **there is no doubt that it is an IO in the second**:
>
>> [. . .] a contagious, sardonic, and unhealthy happiness that made **Cristico** uncomfortable and delighted his mother (Herrera Luque, *Casa*); It is a fight that perhaps makes **many uncomfortable**, but it is an authentic fight (Excélsior 1/9/2000).

Readers remember from Chapter 1 that our understanding of subject in sentences like <u>Ángela</u> estudió '<u>Ángela</u> studied' and *los impuestos aumentaron* 'taxes increased' hides an important distinction: Ángela is the "<u>studier</u>" (student) but taxes are the **increased** (**verbed**). The notions of DO and IO have also made it difficult to distinguish one from the other. RAE is not alone in their difficulty to distinguish whether some objects are direct or indirect. However, we will see that with the **verbed** entailment, it is possible to determine unequivocally that both segments underlined in *que incomodaba **a Cristico** y deleitaba **a su madre**; Es una lucha que quizá le incomode **a muchos*** are DOs. Both objects admit the syntactic alternations (variations) in (1b-h) on the left column in Table 2.1. The corresponding sentences with the verb *importar* 'matter' on the right column admit only the alternations in (2f,i).[4] *A muchos* is uncontroversially an IO with *importar*, but it is a DO with *incomodar* 'make uncomfortable' (and with *deleitar* 'to delight'). Table 2.2 is a translation into English of the sentences in Table 2.1.

10 Distinguishing direct from indirect objects can be a puzzle

Table 2.1 *Incomodar* has <u>verber</u> and **verbed**; *importar* has **verbed** and <u>verbee</u>

<u>Verber</u>, **verbed** *(Sentence 1)*	*Verbed*, <u>verbee</u> *(sentence 2)*
(1)	(2)
a. <u>La lucha</u> (les) incomoda **a muchos**.	a. **La lucha** <u>les</u> importa <u>a muchos</u>.
b. <u>La lucha</u> incomoda **a muchos**.	b. *La lucha importa a muchos.
c. **Muchos** son (los) incomodados (por la lucha).	c. *Muchos son importados (por la lucha).
d. <u>La lucha</u> es la incomodadora.	d. *La lucha es la importadora.
e. **Muchos** <u>se</u> incomodan.	e. *Muchos se importan.
f. **A muchos** les incomoda <u>la lucha</u>.	f. <u>A muchos</u> <u>les</u> importa **la lucha**.
g. **A muchos los** incomoda <u>la lucha</u>.	g. *A muchos los importa la lucha.
h. **Muchos** están incómodos (incomodados).	h. *Muchos están importados.
i. *La lucha es la incomodada.	i. **La lucha** es la **importada** (what matters [<u>to many</u>]).

Table 2.2 Translation of Table 2.1 into English

<u>Verber</u>, **verbed** *(Sentence 1)*	**Verbed**, <u>verbee</u> *(sentence 2)*
(1')	(2')
a. <u>The fight</u> makes **many** uncomfortable.	a. **The fight** matters <u>to many</u>.
b. <u>The fight</u> makes **many** uncomfortable.	b. *The fight matters many.
c. **Many** are made uncomfortable by the fight.	c. *Many are mattered by the fight.
d. <u>The fight</u> is the uncomfortable-er. (i.e. is the maker uncomfortable; the thing making many uncomfortable)	d. *The fight is the matterer.
e. **Many** became uncomfortable. (**Many** were made uncomfortable.)	e. *Many to themselves matter.
f. **To many**, the fight makes **them**[DAT in form] uncomfortable.	f. <u>To many</u>, **the fight** matters <u>to them</u>.
g. **To many**, the fight makes **them**[ACC] uncomfortable.	g. *Many, the fight matters them.
h. Many are uncomfortable. (Resultative)	h. *Many are mattered (i.e. *are in a state of 'matterhood').
i. *The fight is uncomfortable. (*It is the one that is uncomfortable).	i. **The fight** is the **thing mattered** (i.e. **what matters** <u>to many</u>)

If a contagious, sardonic, and unhealthy happiness *incomodaba a Cristico* 'made Cristico uncomfortable', then *Cristico fue incomodado por una alegría contagiosa, sardónica y malsana* 'Cristico was incommodated by a contagious, sardonic, and unhealthy happiness'. Cristico passes the **verbed** entailment. The *a* is the accusative *a* of Spanish. Passive voice is an uncontroversial test for direct objecthood. If it is true that *Cristico fue incomodado*, then it is also true, (1) that *a Cristico lo* incomodaba <u>una alegría contagiosa, sardónica y malsana</u>; (2) that *Cristico* <u>se</u> incomodó con/por esa alegría; and (3) that *Cristico está incómodo* (i.e. *incomodado*). The **verbed** entailment, passive voice, and the three other alternations (the VERBED TOPICALIZATION in 1g, the INTRANSITIVIZATION WITH SE in 1e, and the RESULTATIVE SENTENCE in 1h) show unequivocally that *a Cristico* is a DO in the first segment. With the **verbed** entailment, it is not only possible to determine whether an object is direct; we can absolutely be sure about that. A **verbed** is TOPICALIZED when it is expressed before the verb. A sentence is INTRANSITIVIZED when its <u>verber</u> is replaced with a reflexive pronoun, as explained in González (2022, Chapter 2). A RESULTATIVE sentence is a sentence that expresses a result. *The door is open* is a resultative sentence in English. Incidentally, *the door was open<u>ED</u>* (*by the wind*) is a sentence in the passive voice. If *a door is open*, this sentence entails that it was opened. The fact that *a door was opened* does not necessarily entail that *it is open*. It could have been opened and then closed.

Let us now turn to the second underlined segment (*es una lucha que quizá le incomode a muchos*).[5] This time, we are comparing *incomodar* with *importar* (1) 'matter to', the latter a verb whose object is an indirect one and never takes a direct object.[6] *Le/les* can never be permutated with *la/las/lo/los* in sentences with *importar* (1). In linguists' parlance, *importar* (1) is an unaccusative verb; that is, a verberless verb (a verb whose subject is the **verbed** and whose only object is a <u>verbee</u>). See González (2021, Chapter 5) for a discussion of the true *gustar* verbs in Spanish (verbs like *importar* 'matter to').

The statement by RAE/ASALE (2009: 2681) that there is no doubt that the underlined segment in the second text is an IO is not correct. It probably comes from the understanding that a participant in a sentence doubled with the IO pronoun (*le/les* for the third person) is a DATIVE (an IO is said to be MARKED with the dative case).[7] As González (2021, Chapter 3) shows for Spanish and several other languages, a **verbed** (a direct object) is often "doubled" with an IO pronoun in the language (and in dozens of other languages) when it is human (more generally, animate), and much more often when the <u>verber</u> is not human (inanimate).[8] When that **verbed** is TOPICALIZED (expressed before the verb), the doubling is mandatory. The use of an IO pronoun (i.e. a <u>verbee</u> pronoun) instead of a DO pronoun (i.e. a **verbed** pronoun) is a rule of dative overriding of the accusative that explains dialectal *leísmo* from central and northern Spain, a form of *leísmo* when both the <u>verber</u> and the **verbed** are animate. That rule also explains GENERAL *LEÍSMO* in all of the Spanish-speaking world when the <u>verber</u> is inanimate and the **verbed** is animate. That is, in fact, a rule that accounts for the marking of a **verbed** (a direct object) as if it were a <u>verbee</u> (an IO) in sentences with a single object when that object is animate in Spanish. Many languages have a similar rule. Catalan, German, Hindi, Latin, Nepalese, Portuguese, Spanish, Yiddish, to mention just a few.

Notice that *les* is optional in (1a), as (1b) shows. However, *les* is mandatory in both (2a) and (2b). Observe also that on the surface, the marker *a* appears to be IO marking, as shown in (1b). Interestingly, when that animate **verbed** is expressed preverbally (TOPICALIZED), a duplicating pronoun is mandatory. By dative overriding (González 2021: 31), the pronoun is overwhelmingly the IO pronoun (instead of the DO pronoun). That observation has led many scholars to believe that the presence of the marker *a* is IO marking **and** DO marking (Aissen 2003: 446; Aranovich [Roberto] 2011: 99; Bossong 1991: 158, 2021: 30; RJ Cuervo [1847] 1941: 114; Fábregas 2013: 5, 11, 32; García 1975: 336; Laca 2006: 427; among many others). The grammaticality of (1g) vis-à-vis the ungrammaticality of (2g) is clear evidence that accusative (DO) marking and dative (IO) marking share the marker *a*. However, *le(s)* is the marker of IO and *la(s)*, *lo(s)* is the marker of DO. In other words, an animate DO and any IO share the marker *a* that indicates that the participant is NOT the verber. *Le/les* distinguishes the verbee from the **verbed** when **verbed** and verbee are different. When the **verbed** = verbee, that participant is really a **verbed**, and the subject is always the verber, as the following section shows.

This section has shown that it is possible to determine unequivocally whether an object is direct or indirect with the verber entailment and with the **verbed** entailment. A false verbee is an object that passes the **verbed** entailment, can passivize, and that also allows the alternations in (1b-h). The following section explains false verbees in detail. Keep in mind that verbees can passivize in English (Mandela was given **the Nobel Peace Prize**), but Spanish allows passivization of **verbeds** only (**El Premio Nóbel de la Paz** le fue dado a Mandela; *Mandela fue dado el Premio Nóbel de la Paz). Therefore, a participant that can be passivized in Spanish is a **verbed,** not a verbee.

2.3 False verbees, true verbees, dialectal *leísmo*, and general *leísmo*: everything is connected

Most of those familiar with *leísmo* have heard about dialectal *leísmo*; that is, the use of *le* instead of *lo* in examples like the following. Observe that both the verber and the **verbed** are animate (human).

(3) a. ¿*Viste*   *a Isabel*   *y*   *a Fernando?*
saw-you.NOM to Isabel.ACC and to Fernando.ACC[9]
'Did you see Isabelle and Fernando?'
b. **La** *vi*   *a ella,*   *pero no lo*   *vi*
her.ACC saw-I.NOM to her.ACC but not him.ACC saw-I.NOM
a él.
to him.ACC
'I saw her, but I did not see him'.

c. ***La*** *vi* ***a ella,*** *pero no **le*** *vi*
   her.ACC saw-I.NOM to her.ACC but not him.DAT saw-I.NOM
   a él.
   to him.ACC
   (him.DAT is dative in form. It is ACC in meaning.)
   Same translation as above.

d. ??*Le* *vi* ***a ella,*** *pero no **le*** *vi*
   her.DAT saw-I.NOM to her.ACC but not him.DAT saw-I.NOM
   a él.
   to him.ACC
   (Lit: 'her, I saw to her; but him, I did not see to him'.)

Le is widely accepted for *lo*, but *le* is much more infrequently used for *la* in sentences like those in (3). As RAE/ASALE (2010: 316) put it, "El leísmo de persona femenino (tipo B) está mucho menos extendido, carece de prestigio y se considera incorrecto" ('*Leísmo* referring to a feminine referent (type B) is much less extended, lacks prestige, and it is considered incorrect'. Translation by this author). Dialectal *leísmo* is mostly restricted to a masculine, singular referent (Alcina & Blecua 1975: 606; Fernández-Ordóñez 1999: 1319, 1386; Fernández Ramírez 1987: 43–44; Lapesa 1983: 405–406; Marcos Marín 1978: 45; RAE 1973: 204–205; RAE/ASALE 2010: 316; among many others).[10] Interestingly, most of the cases of dialectal *leísmo* have a verber that is animate. The use and acceptance of *le* for *lo*, but the absence of *le* for *la* when the verber is animate probably comes from statements like the one just quoted from RAE. It is true that most speakers often respect this rule. Some teachers of Spanish will accept *le* for *lo*, but others might not accept *le* for *la*. They might notice it, and they will probably remember that dialectal *leísmo* is presumably restricted to a direct object that is masculine and singular. It is true that *le* for *la* is rarely used when the **verbed** is animate and the verber is also animate. However, when the verber is inanimate, *leísmo* is the rule in 22 out of 22 Spanish-speaking countries.

Table 2.3 Molestar, sorprender, preocupar, acusar, maltratar, and *golpear* pronominalized with an IO pronoun (*les*) and with a DO pronoun (*las*)

A las mujeres les molesta =	17,700	A las mujeres las molesta =	1
A las mujeres les sorprende =	18,000	A las mujeres las sorprende =	2
A las mujeres les preocupa =	21,200	A las mujeres las preocupa =	0
A las mujeres les acusan =	0	A las mujeres las acusan =	7
A las mujeres les maltratan =	0	A las mujeres las maltratan =	1,070
A las mujeres les golpean =	10	A las mujeres las golpean =	4,560

Google search done in December 2021. Each string was searched using double quotation marks (e.g. "a las mujeres les molesta")

14 *Distinguishing direct from indirect objects can be a puzzle*

Table 2.3 above shows the use of *le/les* as opposed to *la/las* with six verbs. The first three verbs are verbs commonly listed as PSYCHOLOGICAL VERBS.[11] The other three are more "physical" verbs. The object of all these verbs is animate. The subject of the first three can be inanimate; the subject of the last three is often animate. *Golpear* 'hit' is interesting because things can also hit people, both physically and figuratively. *Maltratar* 'mistreat' can be used in a physical sense as well as in a psychological one.

Table 2.4 below shows *preocupar* 'worry' preceded by a DO and an IO pronoun and followed by *la*. It is reasonable to assume that *la* overwhelmingly refers to an inanimate verber.

Assuming that *la* after the verb refers to an inanimate verber, Table 2.4 shows the extent of general *leísmo*. The 7,170 vs. 2,710 shows almost three times more mentions for men than for women (72.57% vs. 27.43%, if we consider 7,170 vs. 2,710). The statement that *les* is not as frequent as *le* (Fernández-Ordóñez 1999: 1319; Fernández Ramírez 1987: 43–44; Lapesa 1983: 406; Marcos Marín 1978: 43, 136; RAE/ASALE 2010: 316) might be true for dialectal *leísmo*. It is not true for general *leísmo*. It is impossible to tell apart men from women in a statement like *les incomoda a muchos* 'it makes a lot of people uncomfortable', for example. Indeed, the frequency of *les* with *preocupar* is more remarkable when one thinks that many *les* are expressed with *le*, presumably when the **verbed** is singular. Observe these examples, the first from RAE. Examples (4c-e) are quoted in Marcos Marín (1978: 267):

(4) a. *Es una lucha que quizá **le** incomode **a muchos**.* (Excélsior 1/9/2000, quoted in RAE/ASALE 2010: 2681.)[12]
   b. *Le compré **un libro** a los chicos.* (Belloro 2007: 13)
   c. *Los franciscanos de Perusa le piden a los cristianos ricos **que reúnan un fondo común**.* (E. Montes, 12-V-74)
   d. *Uno nacido en Zaragoza, en la ciudad cesárea augusta, le pone **blancas y rojas coronas martiriales, sacrosantas**, a los himnos de la paganía.* (E. Montes, 13-1-74)
   e. *Es indispensable explicarle a los españoles y estudiar todas las Monarquías.* (28-IV-74)

Table 2.4 Preocupar 'worry' with an IO pronoun (*le/les*) and with a DO pronoun (*la/las, lo/los*)

"La preocupa la" =	2,710 (0.75%)	"Las preocupa la" = 1,020 (0.71%)
"lo preocupa la" =	7,170 (2.34%)	"los preocupa la" = 978 (0.68%)
"le preocupa la" =	348,000 (97.23%)	"les preocupa la" = 141,000 (98.6%)

Google search done in December 2021.

As RJ Cuervo ([1847]1941: 114) observed, "Acaso por esto nos inclinamos a poner en dativo el pronombre con una multitud de verbos cuando el sujeto es de cosa..." ('Perhaps because of this we are inclined to use a dative pronoun with a multitude of verbs when the subject is inanimate'. Translation by this author). Perhaps because most scholars have confined themselves to examples in which only a referent that is singular and masculine was used, RJ Cuervo did not realize that his observation would lead to countless cases of *leísmo* for feminine referents, regardless of number, when the subject is inanimate. That phenomenon is called GENERAL *LEÍSMO* in González (1997, 2021: 31). What is more interesting than dialectal *leísmo* is the observation that when the subject is inanimate, we see GENERAL *LEÍSMO* in 22 out of 22 Spanish-speaking countries, and that *leísmo* applies regardless of the gender and number of the DO. In fact, general *leísmo* is a rule of hundreds of languages. That is the rule observed in PSYCH VERBS; roughly speaking, verbs whose object is animate. When the subject is inanimate, psych verbs tend to mark their single object as if it were an IO instead of a DO. That is, they are topicalized (expressed before the verb) or pronominalized (replaced with a pronoun) with *le/les* instead of *la/las/lo/los*.

González (2021: 34) observes that perhaps the most convincing reason for *leísmo* was that the series *le/lo/lo* (dative/accusative/neuter) does not contrast as well as the series *le/la/lo* (dative/accusative/neuter), as Fernández Ramírez (1987: 43–44) proposed. The problem is that when *le* replaces *lo* for a masculine singular referent, we end up with the same lack of contrast: *le/le/lo* (dative/accusative/neuter).

Vázquez Rozas (2006: 103) observes that there are at least 61 verbs in Spanish that admit accusative (DO) or dative (IO) marking when there is just one object in a sentence. If the verb can mark its single object with the accusative (as a DO), that object is the **verbed**, and the sentence is TRANSITIVE. If that **verbed** is animate (and particularly if the verber is inanimate), that object looks to the speaker as a "verbee", and the sentence would be "INTRANSITIVE". Interestingly, there is no difference in meaning. This is a transitivity paradox explained in González (2021, Chapter 3).

All of the following verbs in Vázquez Rozas (2006: 103) can mark their object with accusative (take a DO, topicalize it with *la/las/lo/los*) or with dative (take an IO, topicalize it with *le/les*): *abrumar, aburrir,* **admirar***, afectar, afligir, alegrar,* angustiar*, apasionar, apenar, asombrar, asustar, atemorizar, aterrar, aterrorizar, atormentar, atraer, avergonzar, cansar, complacer, consolar, convencer,* decepcionar*, deleitar, desanimar, descontentar,* desconsolar*, desesperar, disgustar, distraer,* **divertir***, emocionar, entretener, entristecer, entusiasmar, escandalizar, espantar, estorbar, exasperar, fascinar, fastidiar, favorecer, halagar, impresionar, incomodar, inquietar, interesar, intranquilizar, intrigar, irritar, maravillar, molestar, obsesionar, ofender, pasmar, perjudicar, preocupar, reconfortar, satisfacer, seducir, sorprender, tranquilizar.*

This is, in fact, a subset of the so-called PSYCHOLOGICAL VERBS. The *amuse (frighten)* verbs in Levin (1995: 38) are 220 verbs. *Admirar* 'admire', *apasionar* 'feel passionate about', and *desconsolar* 'distress' are some of the verbs not found in Levin (1995: 38). The point of the last two sentences is to show that lists of verbs are not helpful for most purposes. The equivalent of the 220 *frighten* verbs should behave like the 61 verbs above. Thus, this list is incomplete. So is Levin's list, if it is missing at least three of these verbs. Rather than a list, the best way of describing the behavior of any set of verbs is to discover the rule that allows a group of verbs like the ones in the preceding list to mark its single object as if it were an IO (dative) or a DO (accusative). In this case, this is one "type" of several possible types of psychological verbs. The generalization is that the *admire* class and these 61 verbs require or accept an animate object, and that object is a true **verbed** that looks like a verbee. A false verbee is a **verbed** (always animate!) that can behave as the object of *incomodar* 'make uncomfortable' and *deleitar* 'delight' in the examples by RAE/ASALE (2010) discussed at the beginning of this chapter. A true verbee is a benefactee or malefactee that does not pass the **verbed** entailment because another participant in the sentence passes it. That is true of sentences with verber, **verbed**, and verbee, as in (5a,b) and of verberless sentences; that is, sentences with only a **verbed** and a verbee, as in (5e).

(5) a. We sent **our children** to Grandma.
 b. We sent Grandma **our children**.
 c. #We sent Grandma to our children. (Not entailed by 5a,b)
 d. This university owns **this computer**.
 e. **This computer** belongs to this university.
 f. *This computer belongs this university.

It is uncontroversial that if (5a) is true, (5b) is true. It is also uncontroversial that if (5a) is true, (5c) cannot be true. If sentences with the verb *belong* had verber and **verbed**, speakers of English would say sentences similar to (5f). They do not. Table 2.5 shows true verbees on the left column and false verbees on the right column.

Thus, a false verbee is a **verbed** that is marked as if it were a verbee. It is a DO that looks like an IO. False verbees are overwhelmingly animate.

Once we can distinguish false verbees, it is clear why they look like verbees. The same pattern of marking an animate object as an IO instead of marking it as a DO is a cross-linguistic phenomenon. When that object passes the **verbed** entailment (an entailment that the object of verbs like *gustar* do not pass), then that object is a **verbed**, not a true verbee. González (2021, Chapter 4) identified eleven VERBERLESS verbs in English: (*appeal*(1), *appear, be, belong, cost, happen, matter, occur, remain, seem, sound*(1).[14] He also identified 40 VERBERLESS verbs in Spanish (Chapter 5). On the other hand, the number of verbs that can take an animate **verbed** and will therefore admit *le/les* to replace (or double) its single object is in the hundreds, perhaps in the thousands.

Table 2.5 The difference between true verbees and false verbees (**verbeds**)

A TRUE verbee:	A FALSE verbee:
• The verbee ≠ **verbed** • Never passes the **verbed** entailment. • The IO (*to Grandma*) = PRIMARY object (*Grandma*).[13] It can be topicalized ONLY with *le/les*. • Another participant in the sentence passes the **verbed** entailment. • Verbee = benefactee (or malefactee)	• The verbee = **verbed** • A false verbee passes the **verbed** entailment. • There is only one object. It can be topicalized with *le/les* OR with *la/las/lo/los*. • The subject of a sentence with a false verbee passes the verber entailment. • The verbee = **verbed**
addressee ≠ se**NT** message awardee ≠ award**ED** prize grantee ≠ grant**ED** money licensee ≠ licens**ED** product lessee ≠ leas**ED** property patentee ≠ patent**ED** invention payee ≠ pa**ID** salary When postverbal, a TRUE VERBEE is "duplicated" with an IO pronoun (*le/les*) but not with a DO pronoun (*la/las/lo/los*).	appointee = **appointed (citizen)** detainee = **detained (person)** divorcee = **divorced (spouse)** huggee = **hugged (friend)** interviewee = **interviewed (applicant)** nominee = **nominated (citizen)** tutee = **tutored (learner)** When postverbal, a **verbed** can be "duplicated" in a sentence with an IO pronoun (*le/les*) but not with a DO pronoun (*la/las/lo/los*), except for a few animate **verbeds** in River Plate Spanish.

Wirnsberger (2006: 6), among others, wonders whether the semantic role of **a su amiga** 'her (female) friend' is the same, in both (6a) and (6b).[15]

(6) a. *El chico*   abrazó **a su amiga**.
    the boy.NOM hugged to his friend-FEM.ACC
    'The boy hugged **his friend**'.
b. *El chico*   *le*   dio **un abrazo**   *a su amiga*.
    the boy.NOM her.DAT gave a hug.ACC to his friend-FEM.DAT
    'The boy gave **a hug** to his friend'.

Wirnsberger's question is a problem for a grammar based on subject, DO, and IO as well as for grammars that need to invoke semantic roles (agent, theme, experiencer, goal, recipient, etc.). His question is not a problem for a grammar based on verber and **verbed**, the only two roles needed in González (2021).[16] With verber and **verbed**, there is no need for semantic roles to be defined and told apart from each other. Verber and **verbed** are distinguished from each other with two simple entailments. Regarding (6a,b), speakers of the language do not have any trouble in understanding and producing either sentence or both. They know intuitively and implicitly that in (6a) the boy is the hugger and his friend is **the huggee** (a false verbee). In (6b), the boy is the giver, a hug is the **given**, and his friend is the givee. Speakers know intuitively that hugging **someone** or giving <u>someone</u> **a hug** (or giving **a hug** <u>to someone</u>) are different ways of stating the same event. Most speakers do not even realize that there are at least three different ways of stating this sentence. Any given speaker will intuitively go for one of them and might not even think about the two other choices.

The pattern in (6a,b) is, in fact, very productive. RJ Cuervo ([1847]1941: 114–115) pointed out the existence of pairs like <u>Eso</u> **la** *fatiga*, <u>eso</u> <u>le</u> da *fatiga* '<u>that</u> tires **her**, <u>that</u> causes <u>her</u> **tiredness**; <u>such a thing</u> honors **them**, <u>such a thing</u> gives **honor** <u>to them</u>'; etc. Consider these sentences:

(7) a. <u>Rosa</u> besó **a Pedro**.   (*Besadora* and ***besado***)[17]
    '<u>Rosa</u> kissed **Peter**'.   (<u>Kisser</u> and kissee. Kissee = **kissed**)
  b. <u>Rosa</u> <u>le</u> dio **un beso** <u>a Pedro</u>.   (*dadora*, ***dado***, and *datario*. *Datario* = *beneficiario*)
    '<u>Rosa</u> gave **a kiss** <u>to Peter</u>'.   (<u>giver</u>, **given**, and <u>givee</u>. **Given** ≠ <u>givee</u>)
  c. <u>Rosa</u> <u>le</u> agradeció <u>a Pedro</u>.   (cf. *Rosa lo agradeció a Pedro).
    '<u>Rosa</u> thanked <u>Peter</u>'.
  d. <u>Rosa</u> <u>le</u> dio **las gracias** <u>a Pedro</u>.
    '<u>Rosa</u> gave **her thanks** <u>to Peter</u>'.
  e. *Rosa golpeó **a Pedro**.*
    '<u>Rosa</u> hit **Peter**'.
  f. *Rosa <u>le</u> dio **un golpe** <u>a Pedro</u>.*
    '<u>Rosa</u> gave **a blow** <u>to Peter</u>'.

Observe the different pattern and the contribution of the IO in the following examples:

(8) a. ??Rosa pagó a Pedro.
    '<u>Rosa</u> paid <u>Peter</u>'. (In English, it is understood that <u>she</u> paid <u>him</u> **some money**, not that he was given as payment).
  b. *<u>Rosa</u> <u>le</u> pagó <u>a Pedro</u>.*
    '<u>Rosa</u> paid <u>Pedro</u> [**some money**]'.
  c. *<u>Rosa</u> <u>le</u> pagó **el dinero** <u>a Pedro</u>.*
    '<u>Rosa</u> paid **the money** <u>to Peter</u>'.
  d. ??Rosa pegó a Pedro.
  e. *<u>Rosa</u> <u>le</u> pegó <u>a Pedro</u>.*
    '<u>Rosa</u> hit <u>Peter</u>'. (Lit: <u>Rosa</u> hit [**a blow**] to Peter.)
  f. *<u>Rosa</u> <u>le</u> pegó **un golpe** <u>a Pedro</u>.*
  g. ??Rosa sirvió a Pedro.
  h. *<u>Rosa</u> <u>le</u> sirvió <u>a Pedro</u>.*
    '<u>Rosa</u> served <u>Peter</u> [**his meal**]'.
  i. *<u>Rosa</u> <u>le</u> sirvió **la comida** <u>a Pedro</u>.*
    '<u>Rosa</u> served **his meal** <u>to Peter</u>.

Let us finish with an example from Gutiérrez Ordóñez (1999: 1883) that shows the difficulty in distinguishing a DO from an IO if we use DO and IO. I have added (9c-f).

(9) a. *Los chistes   les   divirtieron a los alumnos.*
    the jokes.NOM them.DAT amused   to the students-MASC.ACC
    'The jokes amused the students'.
  b. *Los alumnos   fueron divertidos por los chistes.*
    the students-MASC.NOM were amused by the jokes
    '**The (male) students** were amused by the jokes'.
  c. *Los chistes   divirtieron a las alumnas.*
    the jokes.NOM amused   to the students-FEM.ACC
    'The jokes amused **the (female) students**'.
  d. *A las alumnas   les   /las   divirtieron*
    to the students-FEM.ACC them.DAT /them.ACC amused
    los chistes.
    the jokes.NOM
    '**The (female) students**, the jokes amused **them**'. (An attempt to mirror in English the topicalization in Spanish in 9d.)
  e. *Las alumnas   se   divirtieron con los chistes.*
    the students-FEM.NOM se.REFL amused   with the jokes
    '**The (female) students** were/got amused by/with/because of the jokes'.
  f. *Las alumnas   están divertidas.* (Resultative sentence)
    the students-FEM.NOM are   amused.
    '**The (female) students** are amused'. (i.e. they are in a state of amusement.)

Gutiérrez Ordóñez (1999: 1883) observes that a sentence like (9a) might be the only sentence with an IO in Spanish that admits the passive voice, as in (9b). All the sentences whose single object is animate, but whose object passes the **verbed** entailment will accept passive voice and all the alternations in (1b-h). That includes not only the 61 verbs in Vázquez Rozas (2006: 103) but also hundreds and perhaps thousands of verbs that admit an animate object. In fact, it is easier to state which verbs it does not include: the verberless verbs in Spanish, which are approximately 40 (González 2021, Chapter 5). Those verbs can never replace (or "double") their object with a DO (**verbed**) pronoun.

(10) a. *A las alumnas   les   gustaron los chistes.*
    to the students-FEM.DAT them.DAT liked   the jokes.NOM
    "The female students liked the jokes'.
  b. **A las alumnas las gustaron los chistes.*

Observe that (9a) not only admits the passive voice. It admits, of course, the omission of *les* in (9c), which shows that the sentence is clearly transitive. In addition, it admits *las* when the **verbed** is topicalized, as in (9d), as well as the intransitivization with *se* in (9e), two alternations that confirm that the sentence is transitive. Finally, it admits the RESULTATIVE alternation, another test for **verbedhood**, as the discussion of *incomodar* and *matter to* showed above in Table 2.1.

Table 2.6 How "**a Margarita**" (verbed) is different from "a Margarita" (verbee)

(*Ellas*) Invitaron **a Margarita**. (They invited **Margarita**.)	(*Ellas*) Le hicieron **un pastel** a Margarita. (They made **a cake** for Margarita.)
Invitaron **a Margarita**. **A Margarita** la/??le invitaron. *Margarita fue invitada* (*por ellas*). *Margarita se invitó*. (**She** invited herself or **she** was invited. *La invitaron* [they invited **her**]). *Margarita está* **invitada**. *Margarita es la* **invitada**. (**Margarita** is the verbed).	??Hicieron un pastel a Margarita. *A Margarita* ???la/*le hicieron* **un pastel**. ????Margarita fue hecha un pastel. #*Margarita se hizo* **un pastel**. (Margarita baked herself **a cake**.) #Margarita está hecha. #Margarita es la hecha. (cf. **El pastel** es **el hecho**.) (Margarita is the verbee).

??: a marginal sentence. Very few speakers will utter it.
???: a very marginal sentence.
????: a very, very marginal sentence.
#: a grammatical sentence, but a sentence not entailed by the sentence under discussion (*Le hicieron* **un pastel** a Margarita).

Table 2.6 shows the difference between *a Margarita* as a **verbed** and as a verbee.

This section has shown that false verbees are animate objects that pass the **verbed** entailment. They are DOs that are marked as if they were IOs. Now readers understand better how the notion of subject and DO, which blurs the distinction between verber and **verbed** in sentences with just a subject (*Ángela worked*; *taxes increased*) also blurs the distinction between DO and IO, as the quote from RAE/ASALE (2009: 2681) at the beginning of this chapter shows.

Distinguishing some DOs from some IOs is "not possible", even for scholars, if we try to do so with DO and IO. Distinguishing a **verbed** from a verbee is a simple entailment that children "know" because it is part of universal grammar. Children can understand and produce sentences in the passive voice a couple of years before they start elementary school, evidence that they distinguish a subject that is the **verbed**, not the verber. Snyder & Hyams (2015) have reported that Italian children use the auxiliary *essere* 'be' consistently and accurately at the age of two years and one month with many verbs in Italian that take that auxiliary. As shown in González (2021, Chapter 2), sentences whose subject is the **verbed** (or the verbee) take *essere* 'be', not *avere* 'have'. That is clear evidence that Italian children can tell whether the subject is the verber or the **verbed**. They do so intuitively and implicitly, as we all do in our regular use of language. If children can "tell" whether the subject is a verber or a **verbed**, they can also distinguish the **verbed** from the verbee. The analysis of intransitivization with *se* ("reflexivization") in González (2021, Chapter 2, 2022) is evidence that indeed children do distinguish them.

2.4 In the classroom

The exercises below are ideas on how to present and practice these concepts with students. Exercises can be adapted in different ways. Teachers can replace some of the sentences and use sentences found in the readings in the materials they are using in class. That way, they are using better those materials, and they will be connecting them to the real world and adapting them to their students' experiences, making them more meaningful. These sample exercises are meant to show how exercises should look like when verber and **verbed** are used in the classroom.

Here are some additional ideas. First, an effective way of introducing verber, **verbed**, and verbee is by using the three variations of sentence (11a), as in (11b-d), and asking learners to determine who/what is the buyer, who/what is the **bought**, and who is the benefactee (verbee).

(11) a. We bought **new pajamas** for our children.
 b. We bought our children **new pajamas**.
 c. **New pajamas** were bought for our children (by us).
 d. Our children were bought **new pajamas** (by us).

Students will not have any problem in completing this task. Teachers can point out that *for our children* is the IO in (11a,c), the PRIMARY object in (11b), and the subject in (11d). However, (for) our children is always the benefactee; that is, the participant getting the **verbed**. **New pajamas** is the direct object in (11a), the SECONDARY object in (11b), and the subject in (11c). *We* are, of course, the buyers. When the verber is demoted to a *by phrase* (or left out altogether), the **verbed** is promoted to subject. That is passive voice, as in (11c). English also allows the promotion of an IO to subject, as in (11d), but with a difference: the **verbed** must also appear in the sentence, as (12c) shows. If (11a) is true, only two of the following strings are true:

(12) a. **New pajamas** were bought.
 b. #Our children were bought.
 c. Our children were bought **new pajamas** (by us).

Any speaker of English knows that the string in (12b) is incomplete, and that what was bought must be indicated after *was bought*, as in (12c). That is exactly what native (and L2) speakers of English do.

After the preceding example, students should be ready for a more abstract one. Now students themselves will be able to point out how verber, **verbed**, and verbee are constant, but the traditional grammatical functions (subject, DO, IO) vary in any alternation of (13a).

(13) a. We sent **our children** to Grandma.
   b. We sent Grandma **our children**.
   c. **Our children** were sent to Grandma.
   d. Grandma was sent **our children**.

Students will also be able to tell the difference in meaning in (14a,b), and why only one of them is true if (13a) is true.

(14) a. We sent our children **Grandma**.
   b. We sent Grandma **our children**.

Sentence (14b) is the only sentence that is true if (13a) is true.

Second, the following examples are similar to examples discussed in Wasow (1977). Observe that in a purported sale event in which an item did not get sold, that item can be referred to as the **unsold** (15e), but the sellee cannot be referred to as the "unsold-ee".

(15) a. We did not sell **a truck** to Uncle Eduardo.
   b. We did not sell Uncle Eduardo **a truck**.
   c. **A truck** was not sold to Uncle Eduardo.
   d. Uncle Eduardo was not sold **a truck**.
   e. **An unsold truck**.
   f. #The unsold Uncle Eduardo.

The point is, of course, that a **verbed** allows to be paraphrased as an **unverbed**, but the verbee does not. That is a test for direct objecthood vis-à-vis indirect objecthood.

Third, depending on the level of the class, teachers might use Bresnan (1982: 23–31) past-participle adjective conversion rule. Bresnan observed that the past participle of a verb (*wilted* and *grown* in 16a,b below) can modify as an adjective the **verbed** (an internal/direct-object-like argument in Chomskyan linguistics and in other theories), but not the verber (the external/agentive argument in theories before the verber, **verbed** theory):

(16) a. **The flowers** wilted → the wilted **flowers**.
   b. The farmer grew **potatoes** → the grown **potatoes**; #the grown farmer.

Fourth, teachers can also take advantage of Table 2.1, repeated here as Table 2.6, to have their learners practice verbs whose single object is marked as a verbee, but which it is really a **verbed**. Any of the 61 verbs in Vázquez

Table 2.7 Incomodar has verber, verbed; importar has verbee, verbed

Verber, verbed (Sentence 1)	Verbed, verbee (sentence 2)
(1)	(2)
a. La lucha (les) incomoda **a muchos**.	a. **La lucha** les importa a muchos.
b. La lucha incomoda **a muchos**.	b. *La lucha importa a muchos.
c. **Muchos** son (los) incomodados (por la lucha).	c. *Muchos son importados (por la lucha).
d. La lucha es la incomodadora.	d. *La lucha es la importadora.
e. **Muchos** se incomodan.	e. *Muchos se importan.
f. **A muchos** les incomoda la lucha.	f. A muchos les importa **la lucha**.
g. **A muchos** los incomoda la lucha.	g. *A muchos los importa la lucha.
h. **Muchos** están incómodos (incomodados).	h. *Muchos están importados.
i. *La lucha es la incomodada.	i. **La lucha** es la **importada (the fight** is what matters [to many]).

Rozas (2006: 103) will behave like *incomodar* below. A true *verberless* verb (*aparecer* 'appear', *costar* 'cost', *doler* 'hurt', *ocurrir* 'happen', *pertenecer* 'belong', etc.), will behave like *importar* 'matter to'. The only object of the former verbs (Vázquez Rozas 61 verbs) is a **verbed**, which looks like a verbee. Crucially, the other participant will be the verber. The only object of the latter verbs (*aparecer, costar,* etc.) is a verbee. Crucially, the other participant will be the **verbed**.

Linguists and teachers will realize that the preceding table amounts to a way of presenting evidence, as linguists do. An important difference is that most learners will be able to see most of the points in the preceding table. Beginning learners will be able to recognize at least the passive voice in (1c). Stating that sentence in the past tense might help beginners that would need some help. In Spanish, passive voice is relatively infrequent in the present tense.

I have taken the harder route and offered suggestions for English. Distinguishing a **verbed** from a verbee in Spanish should be somewhat easier, with a caveat. That task is relatively easy if we have two objects. The reason is that Spanish allows dative shift, but the preposition is not dropped.

(17) a. [Yo] *Le* compré/di/mandé/prometí **un hermoso ramo**
 I.NOM her-DAT bought/gave/sent/promised a   beautiful bouquet
 de flores *a mi esposa.*
 of flowers to my wife.DAT
 'I bought/gave/sent/promised **a beautiful bouquet of flowers** for/to my wife'.
 b. *[Yo] Le* compré/di/mandé/prometí *a mi esposa* **un hermoso ramo de flores**.
 'I bought/gave/sent/promised my wife **a beautiful bouquet of flowers**'.

The complication is that when there is only one object, and that object has a "doubling" IO pronoun or is pronominalized with an IO pronoun, we have the difficulty encountered by RAE/ASALE (2009: 2681) in §2.2 above. This chapter has shown that the **verbed** entailment solves that difficulty.

I will leave it here. These suggestions should be enough for teachers to write exercises of their own. Indeed, since this is a new proposal, we can expect that textbook writers will rethink explanations and exercises. It is in those textbooks and materials that more communicative and better contextualized practice can be proposed. This is an invitation to improve teaching materials, not only in Spanish but in many other languages. Particularly languages with a robust verbee (IO). Several of the most commonly taught L2 languages in the world are robust verbee users.

2.5 Conclusions

This chapter distinguishes true verbees from false verbees with a simple entailment that true verbees do not pass, but that false verbees do pass.

First, a true verbee is a benefactee (or a malefactee) in a sentence with a verber and a **verbed**, even when the **verbed** is not explicit, as in *I wrote [to] my Mom*. In an event of writing, Mom can be the writer or the addressee, but no Mom ends up as the written message. Furthermore, even in a sentence like Mandela was given **the Nobel Peace Prize** in 1993, the **given** was, of course, **the Nobel Peace Prize**. Mandela was not given to anyone. Speakers of English can say a sentence like **The Nobel Peace Prize** was given in 1993. However, no speaker of English will say or write that #*Mandela was given in 1993* and stop there. They will invariably add **what** was given to him: *Mandela was given the Nobel Peace Prize in 1993*. Second, the only object of sentences with verberless verbs (*appear, belong, cost, happen, matter, occur, sound*(1), *remain*, etc.) is also a true verbee that always requires the marker *to* (**honesty** matters to responsible citizens; **we** belong to the earth). The **mattered** and **belonged** are ***honesty*** and ***we***. The verbee is different from the **verbed** in the sentence.

False verbees are countless single objects that are topicalized (expressed preverbally), replaced, or "doubled" with a verbee pronoun (*le/les*) instead of (*la/las, lo/los*). Each of those objects passes the **verbed** entailment, the subject of the sentence passes the verber entailment, and they can ALWAYS be "doubled" with a pronoun for the **verbed** (*la/las, lo/los*) as well when topicalized or replaced. *Le/les* may appear in the same sentence with a postverbal **verbed**, particularly when the verber is inanimate. However, a "duplicating" *la/las/lo/los* is extremely infrequent in this case, except perhaps in River Plate Spanish. The "verbee" is the same as the **verbed**.

Interestingly, English also has, in a sense, false verbees. The NOMINALIZATION (the expression of a DO as a NOUN) of an ANIMATE **verbed** NOUN is done with the verbee-forming suffix in English. The past participle of a verb and its corresponding **verbed** can be expressed in English with a single noun that combines them, provided the verbed is ANIMATE: an appointed official = an appointee, a divorced person = a divorcee, a dumped boyfriend or girlfriend = a dumpee, an interviewed candidate = an interviewee, a kissed person = a kissee, a nominated candidate = a nominee, etc. As in Spanish, some of these nominalizations can be traced back to sentences with three participants: an appointee was offered an appointment, an interviewee was given an interview, a huggee was given a hug, etc.

An object topicalized, replaced, or "doubled" with an IO pronoun (*le/les*) is not always a verbee, as the **verbed** entailment unequivocally shows. Therefore, when we use *le/les* as the mark of indirect objecthood and *la/las/lo/los* as the mark of direct objecthood, it is impossible to distinguish them because DOs and IOs have been inextricably tangled since the early times of Spanish.[18] In fact, the entanglement goes back to Latin and Greek (and perhaps further back), as statements that verbs with two participants "governed" (i.e. required or favored) dative (instead of accusative) in Latin show.[19] Statements like these are common in traditional Spanish grammar (Lapesa 1983: 406; Marcos Marín 1978: 103; among others).

As stated in RAE/ASALE (2009: 2681), it is not possible, even for scholars, to distinguish some DOs from some IOs. That is true if we work with the notions of DO and IO. On the other hand, with the **verbed** entailment, it is possible for college students learning Spanish as a second language to distinguish them. L2 learners of Spanish who know the meaning of the words in Table 2.1 can grasp this point much better than we, as scholars, have grasped it since nominative (subject), accusative (direct object), and dative (IO) began to be used 21 centuries ago. L2 learners can do so by *applying explicitly* two entailments that they know intuitively since they began understanding their native language: the verber entailment and the **verbed** entailment.

2.6 Exercises

Exercise 1. (Answers and some explanation after the exercise)

Identify the verber by underlying it, the **verbed** by drawing a circle around it, and the verbee by a double underline. Sometimes, there is only the verbee pronoun (*me, te, nos, os, le, les*). These sentences come from short stories for children.

- Remember that Spanish strongly favors the omission of the verber, if it is known information. For example: – *Ayer conocí a Estela. ¡Es encantadora!* The sentence ¡*ella es encantadora*! is a sentence that native speakers rarely utter as a comment to the first sentence. The verber is omitted in sentences (7, 8, 9, 10–15) below.

- As with the <u>verber</u>, Spanish also strongly favors the omission of the <u>verbee</u>, if known information. However, the corresponding pronoun for that <u>verbee</u> stays in the sentence, as Chapter 4 shows. There are 13 sentences with a <u>verbee</u> (and/or its corresponding pronoun) out of the following 15 sentences. Ten of those sentences have just the pronoun. The pronoun helps listeners/readers distinguish the <u>verbee</u> from the **verbed**.
- Observe the connection between omitting the <u>verber</u> (more often than not an animate participant, often DEFINITE) and the <u>verbee</u>, likewise more often than not an animate participant who is often DEFINITE. Roughly speaking, a noun is DEFINITE if it is a proper name or if it is preceded by the definite article (*la/las/el/los*). Interestingly, the <u>verbee</u> might be animate more often than the <u>verber</u> is. That is an issue for further research.

  1. La abuela le tocó los ojos al lobo.
  2. El gigante le dio una cama al sastrecillo para que durmiera.
  3. La abuelita le había regalado una capa de color rojo.
  4. La mamá le envió pan y miel.
  5. El mercader le concedió la libertad.
  6. El lobo le indicó el camino.
  7. Tenía grandes virtudes para la costura.
  8. Le indicaré el camino largo.
  9. Tomó el camino.
  10. Les dio golosinas, leche y nueces.
  11. Le dio al muchacho 100 monedas de oro.
  12. Le clavamos una estaca ardiente en su único ojo.
  13. Le hizo muchos y valiosos regalos.
  14. Le agradeció el regalo.
  15. Relataron la historia, la cual a todos les pareció sorprendente.

Answers to exercise 1

Note: the <u>verber</u> will be underlined; the **verbed**, bolded; the <u>verbee</u>, double underlined.

1. <u>La abuela</u> <u>le</u> tocó **los ojos** <u>al lobo</u>.
2. <u>El gigante</u> <u>le</u> dio **una cama** <u>al sastrecillo</u> para que durmiera.
3. <u>La abuelita</u> <u>le</u> había regalado **una capa de color rojo**.
4. <u>La mamá</u> <u>le</u> envió **pan y miel**.
5. <u>El mercader</u> <u>le</u> concedió **la libertad**.
6. <u>El lobo</u> <u>le</u> indicó **el camino**.
7. Tenía **grandes virtudes** para la costura. (<u>Verber</u> = ella/él)
8. <u>Le</u> indicaré **el camino largo**. (<u>Verber</u> = yo)
9. Tomó **el camino**. (<u>Verber</u> = ella)
10. <u>Les</u> dio **golosinas, leche y nueces**. (<u>Verber</u> = ella/él/alguien)

Distinguishing direct from indirect objects can be a puzzle 27

11. Le dio <u>al muchacho</u> **100 monedas de oro**.
12. Le clavamos **una estaca ardiente** en su único ojo. (<u>Verber</u> = nosotros)
13. Le hizo **muchos y valiosos regalos**. (<u>Verber</u> = ella/él/alguien)
14. Le agradeció **el regalo**. (<u>Verber</u> = ella/él/alguien)
15. Relataron **la historia**, la cual <u>a todos les</u> pareció sorprendente. (Interestingly, *la historia* is the **verbed** of *relataron* (<u>ellos</u>). ***La historia*** is also the **verbed** of *pareció*. 'The story seemed surprising <u>to all of them</u>'. *Parecer* 'seem' is like *matter*.). (<u>Verber</u> = ellos/ellas [those telling the story.)

Exercise 2. Answers (and some explanation) after the exercise

The sentences in exercise 1 had a <u>verber</u> and a **verbed**, even if the former was not explicit (expressed in the sentence). Thirteen of them also had a <u>verbee</u> (often just the pronoun for the <u>verbee</u>). The following 15 sentences have just either a <u>verber</u> or a **verbed**, but not both. If it is the <u>verber</u>, underline it; if it is the **verbed**, draw a circle around it. These sentences also come from short stories for children.

1. Mis hermanos trabajarán juntos.
2. El gato corrió hacia un par de campesinos.
3. El conejo azul gritó y gruñó.
4. El conejo azul caminó durante varias horas.
5. La elefanta gritó asustada.
6. Le gritó el conejo azul.
7. El molinero murió.
8. El conejo azul se enfadaba más y más.
9. El sol se ocultó.
10. Nadie cantó aquella mañana a primera hora.
11. Una familia de ratones apareció por allí.
12. Sentenció el domador.
13. Gruñó malhumorado el león.
14. Exclamó contenta la elefanta Amaranta.
15. No podemos competir con ella.

Answers to exercise 2

- Notice that in Spanish, the <u>verber</u> may appear after the verb. Likewise, a **verbed** may appear before the verb.
- The <u>verber</u> is underlined; the **verbed**, bolded.
- Readers who do not readily see why a participant is the **verbed** ("recognizing" a <u>verber</u> is a more intuitive task) should read González (2021), where <u>verber</u>, **verbed**, and <u>verbee</u> are explained in detail. Readers can also come

back to this exercise after reading the rest of this book. Readers might see then a point that they might not be grasping now.

1. Mis hermanos trabajarán juntos.
2. El gato corrió hacia un par de campesinos.
3. El conejo azul gritó y gruñó.
4. El conejo azul caminó durante varias horas.
5. La elefanta gritó asustada.
6. Le gritó el conejo azul.
7. **El molinero** murió. (*El molinero* is the dead; not the "deader".)
8. **El conejo azul** se enfadaba más y más. (A reflexive pronoun [se] indicates that the verber was omitted. The "new" subject is the **verbed**. Something angered **the rabbit**; therefore, **the rabbit** is angered.)
9. **El Sol** se ocultó. (A participant that moves itself is the mover and the **moved**. If *you* move **a chair**, you are the mover and **the chair** is the **moved**. However, if **you** move, you are the mover AND the **moved**. As we loosely express it, the Sun is presumably "the setter" and "the set". That way of conceptualizing the sun as the one moving is pre-Copernican, of course.)
10. Nadie cantó aquella mañana a primera hora.
11. **Una familia de ratones** apareció por allí. (*Aparecer* 'appear' is a verberless verb. If there is only one participant in the sentence, it will be the **appeared**. That participant might appear to someone. Intuitively, *appear* will have just the **verbed** more often than it would have **verbed** and verbee.)
12. Sentenció el domador.
13. Gruñó malhumorado el león.
14. Exclamó contenta la elefanta Amaranta.
15. No podemos competir con ella. ([Nosotros] no podemos competir con ella.)

Exercise 3

Indicate the verber by underlying it, the **verbed** by drawing a circle around it, and the verbee by double underlining it. Please do the same for each pronoun in any of these three roles. The participant might have been omitted. These sentences come from writing by students in college. Eight of these sentences are adapted from "Compensaciones", a short story by Mario Benedetti.

- Remember that *le(les)* is a true verbee pronoun if there is also a **verbed** (different from the referent of *le/les*) in the sentence.
- *Le(les)* is used instead of *lo/los* (and sometimes instead of *la/las*) when the **verbed** is animate (a person, simplifying somewhat). Crucially, the other participant in the sentence is the verber.

1. El muchacho mayor abandonó los estudios a los 17 años.

2. El hermano mayor llamó esa tarde a su otro hermano.
3. Esa tarde les llevó el último disco de Marta Gómez a sus padres.
4. El padre llevaba al niño en los brazos.
5. Los dos hermanos atendieron intermitentemente a la misma noviecita.
6. Decidieron no introducir temas conflictivos en las conversaciones familiares.
7. El hermano menor le llevó sopa a su otro hermano a la cama.
8. Desde ese día, abolieron el tema.
9. Les tenían mucha consideración a la mamá y al papá.
10. Después de la llamada, el hermano menor visitó al mayor.
11. El problema de la semejanza adquirió mucha importancia.
12. A los dos hermanos los/les veíamos cada noche en la discoteca.
13. A las dos hermanas las/les veíamos cada noche en la discoteca.[20]
14. A Allison le aceptaron la propuesta.
15. Le aceptaron la invitación.
16. La aceptaron en todas las universidades a las cuales solicitó.
17. No acepte el paquete si el cliente no permite que lo abra.
18. Ábrales los paquetes a cada uno de los clientes.
19. A Allison le aceptaron en todas las universidades a las cuales solicitó.
20. La militancia le absorbía mucho tiempo.
21. Andaban por caminos tan separados que ya nadie los confundía.
22. Al joven nunca lo detuvieron.
23. El joven se le llevó la chaqueta a su hermano.
24. A Eduardo nunca le detuvieron.
25. A Marta nunca le detuvieron.

Answers to exercise 3. The <u>verber</u> is underlined; the verbed is in bold, and the <u>verbee</u> is double underlined

1. <u>El muchacho mayor</u> abandonó **los estudios** a los 17 años.
2. <u>El hermano mayor</u> llamó esa tarde **a su otro hermano**.
3. Esa tarde <u>les</u> llevó **el último disco de Marta Gómez** <u>a sus padres</u>.
4. <u>El padre</u> llevaba **al niño** en los brazos.
5. <u>Los dos hermanos</u> atendieron intermitentemente **a la misma noviecita**.
6. Decidieron **no introducir temas conflictivos** en las conversaciones familiares.
7. <u>El hermano menor</u> <u>le</u> llevó **sopa** <u>a su otro hermano</u> a la cama.
8. Desde ese día, abolieron **el tema**.
9. <u>Les</u> tenían **mucha consideración** <u>a la mamá y al papá</u>.
10. Después de la llamada, <u>el hermano menor</u> visitó **al mayor**.
11. <u>El problema de la semejanza</u> adquirió **mucha importancia**.
12. **A los dos hermanos los**/les veíamos cada noche en la discoteca.[21]
13. **A las dos hermanas las**/les veíamos cada noche en la discoteca.
14. <u>A Allison</u> <u>le</u> aceptaron **la propuesta**.

15. Le aceptaron **la invitación**.
16. **La** aceptaron en todas las universidades a las cuales solicitó.
17. No acepte (usted) **el paquete** si el cliente no permite que **lo** abra.
18. Ábra<u>les</u> **los paquetes** a cada uno de los clientes.
19. **A Allison le** aceptaron en todas las universidades a las cuales solicitó. (Bolded because Allison is the accepted. This is a false verbee. **A Allison la** aceptaron . . . is probably more frequent.)
20. La militancia le absorbía **mucho tiempo**.
21. Andaban por caminos tan separados que ya nadie **los** confundía.
22. **Al joven** nunca **lo** detuvieron.
23. El joven se le llevó **la chaqueta** a su hermano. (See González 2022, Chapters 2, 3 for an explanation on why *El joven* is the verbee and *se* is replacing the verber.)
24. **A Eduardo** nunca **le** detuvieron. (Bolded because this is dialectal *leísmo*. *Eduardo* is the detained. The detained = the detainee).
25. ??A Marta nunca le detuvieron. > **A Marta** nunca **la** detuvieron. (In a search in Corpes XXI for *le detuvieron*, the first 18 sentences refer to a masculine referent. That masculine referent is a DO, but it is tagged as a "dative". The *le* in sentence 19 (in Corpes XXI) refers to a feminine referent, but it is a true IO (*Micaela y Felicitas le detuvieron las manos*. Searched done in November 2022.). This is clearly an issue for further research.

Exercise 4

Some of the following sentences show some mistakes of **verbed** (DO) or verbee (IO). Correct the mistakes. Some of the sentences are correct. The sentences were written by college students of Spanish as an L2. The main mistake is interpreting a **verbed** as if it were a verbee and using a duplicating pronoun that native speakers do not use if the **verbed** is in postverbal position. When that **verbed** is preverbal, pronoun doubling is mandatory. If that **verbed** is animate, *le/les* is more frequent than *la/las*, *lo/los*, particularly if the verber is inanimate.

Example:
Le extraño mucho **a mi familia**. → Extraño mucho **a mi familia**.
(**A mi familia** is the **verbed**. An overwhelming majority of native speakers does not duplicate a **verbed** when postverbal).[22]

1. Hoy es el día de la graduación y les invitan toda la familia a celebrar en la casa.
2. Les invitamos a todas las personas de la comunidad.
3. Todos se disfrutaron mucho la fiesta.

4. Voy a extrañarles las personas de Cabo Verde porque son muy amables.
5. Un sustantivo le acompaña un adjetivo. (Intended from 5 to 9: an adjective accompanies a noun.)
6. Un sustantivo acompaña un adjetivo.
7. Un adjetivo acompaña un sustantivo.
8. A un sustantivo lo acompaña un adjetivo.
9. A un sustantivo le acompaña un adjetivo.
10. La calma sigue la tormenta.

Answers to exercise 4

1. Hoy es el día de la graduación y les invitan toda la familia a celebrar en la casa. → Hoy es el día de la graduación e invitan a toda la familia a celebrar en la casa.
2. Les invitamos a todas las personas de la comunidad. → Invitamos **a todas las personas de la comunidad**. → Invitamos **a toda la comunidad**. (Así evitamos una palabra redundante en el contexto.)
3. Todos se disfrutaron mucho la fiesta. → Todos disfrutaron mucho **la fiesta**.
4. Voy a extrañarles las personas de Cabo Verde porque son muy amables. → Voy a extrañar **a las personas de Cabo Verde** porque. . . . Also: voy a extrañar **a la gente de Cabo Verde** porque es muy amable.
5. El sustantivo le acompaña el adjetivo. → **Al sustantivo** le acompaña el adjetivo.
6. El sustantivo acompaña el adjetivo. → **Al sustantivo lo** acompaña el adjetivo.
7. El adjetivo acompaña el sustantivo. → El adjetivo acompaña **al sustantivo**.
8. **Al sustantivo lo** acompaña el adjetivo. Correcta.
9. **Al sustantivo** le acompaña el adjetivo. Correcta.
10. La calma sigue la tormenta → La calma sigue **a la tormenta**. Also: **a la tormenta** le/la sigue la calma.

Notes

1 The verber will be underlined; the **verbed**, bolded; and the verbee will be double underlined. These terms are explained in Chapter 1. The equivalent of these terms in Spanish are VERBADORA/VERBADOR, **VERBADA/VERBADO**, and VERBATARIA/VERBATARIO.
2 Key terms will be capitalized when their mention is particularly relevant. If they are not explained in the same paragraph, they will be explained in an endnote. An object (direct or indirect) is TOPICALIZED when it is expressed preverbally, as is *Mandela* in *A Mandela se le dio el Premio Nóbel de la Paz* 'Mandela was given the Nobel Peace Prize'. An IO is presumably DUPLICATED or DOUBLED in the same sentence with its corresponding IO pronoun. Chapter 4 shows that the pronoun does not "double" the IO, but rather that the IO can be deleted when it is known information. The IO pronoun is "generated" together with the IO, but the former stays in the sentence whereas the latter is often dropped.

3 An asterisk (*) before a sentence means that native speakers rarely or never produce that sentence. Two questions marks (??) mean that the sentence is marginal (Maldonado [1999]2006: 43).
4 *Importar* 'matter to' (a *gustar* verb) is UNACCUSATIVE (VERBERLESS). That means that it does not have a verber. When there is no verber in a sentence, the **verbed** is promoted to subject (the accusative "unaccusativizes") and is expressed as the NOMINATIVE (the subject) in a sentence. That is, in essence, the same rule that turns a sentence in the active voice into a sentence in the passive voice (*you bought this book* yesterday vs. **this book** was bought yesterday). Since *gustar* verbs are VERBERLESS, the **verbed** unaccusativizes and is expressed as the NOMINATIVE (the subject). The only object of a sentence with a verberless verb is a benefactee or malefactee (*appealee, appearee, belongee, costee, happenee, matteree*, etc.).
5 The lack of number agreement (*le* instead of *les*) is common among native speakers, including writers, as many scholars have observed (Belloro 2015: 80; Company Company 2006: 543–549; García-Miguel 2015; Gutiérrez Ordóñez 1999: 1872; Keniston 1937: 69; Marcos Marín 1978: 79, 267–268; RAE/ASALE 2009: 2664; among many others). See five examples in (4a-e) below. This writer praises students as making a "native speaker mistake" when they do so in speaking or in writing.
6 There are two *importar* verbs in Spanish. *Importar* (1) 'matter to' has **mattered** and matteree (González 2021, chapter 4). *Importar* (2) 'import' is a verb with importer and **imported** (*Many countries import flowers from Colombia*).
7 The IO is always MARKED with *a* (preceded by the marker *a*). As Chapter 4 shows, the marker *a* indicates non verber; that is, **verbed** or verbee. A verbee pronoun (*le/les* for the third person) co-referring with a verbee distinguishes the verbee from the **verbed**. *La/las/los/las* co-refers with the latter, when expressed preverbally.
8 Chapter 4 shows that an IO pronoun does not really "double" the IO. The pronoun is a marker of indirect objecthood (dative case). That is, a "doubling" IO pronoun indicates that the participant with which it co-occurs is MARKED with the DATIVE CASE. When the IO is known information, it is dropped. But we will refer to "doubling" for ease of exposition for now. That move will not affect the main point of this chapter.
9 Abbreviations are as follows: ACC(usative), DAT(ive), FEM(inine), MASC(uline), NOM(inative), REFL(exive) pronoun.
10 It is interesting to notice this observation by Fernández-Ordóñez (1999: 1365):

> La existencia de esta escala de valoración y de corrección progresiva de los usos referenciales debe haber surgido ya desde tiempos pasados, lo que explicaría que siempre fuera el leísmo personal masculino y singular el único empleo abiertamente presente en la lengua escrita.
>
> The existence of this progressive scale of *valoración* (recognizing due value) and correction of the referential uses must have originated a long time ago, which would explain why masculine, singular *leísmo* referring to a person has always been the only use openly present in the written language. (Translation by this author).

11 Roughly speaking, PSYCH(OLOGICAL) VERBS express cognition, emotion, or perception, and the more interesting psych verbs are those whose **verbed** is animate and whose verber is inanimate. *Fear* and *frighten* are two widely discussed psych verbs. Interestingly, if the **verbed** of *astonish* is animate, *astonish* would be a *frighten* verb; if both verber and **verbed** are animate, *astonish* would be a *fear* verb. The research on psych verbs is extensive. Psych transitive verbs tend to mark their **verbed** as if it were a verbee in Spanish and in many other languages.

12 Glosses and translation were not provided when the point is clear from the discussion, and particularly when examples come from literary sources. The coding (underline, **bold**, double underline) provides a new tool that helps readers understand the point of the example without the need for a gloss.
13 The distinction between PRIMARY object and SECONDARY object was proposed in Dryer (1986: 814) for English and for many other languages. An IO is called a PRIMARY object when "dative shifted". The primary object is the benefactee/malefactee (often animate), and it follows the verb without a preposition. The secondary object is the DO (often inanimate), and it follows the primary object. This distinction was widely adopted. The distinction between **verbed** and verbee provides new arguments against Dryer's proposal. As with APPLICATIVES (endnote 15), further discussion of Dryer's proposal is beyond the scope of this book.
14 The verberless verbs in Spanish are the closest equivalents of the class of *piacere* verbs in Italian, as first proposed by Belletti & Rizzi (1988). The 11 verbs in English just mentioned are verbs that favor or require two participants (the **verbed** and the verbee). This list does not include verberless verbs used more often than not with just one participant, like *be born, die, exist, fall*. Verbs of movement are an interesting case. When the **moved** is inanimate, the mover and the **moved** are different (*Alicia moved **the chair*** , where Alicia is the mover and **the chair** is the **moved**). When the only participant is animate, the mover and the **moved** are the same (***Alicia moved***, where Alicia is the mover and the **moved**. *Alicia se movió* in Spanish).
15 Different semantic roles would require the distinction between HIGH and LOW APPLICATIVES, a theoretical distinction beyond the scope of this book. Interested readers are referred to MC Cuervo (2003, 2020 and references therein) and Pylkkänen (2008), among many others.
16 The verbee is interpreted by putting together the meaning of the marker *a* plus the noun phrase (=DP) following it, as with any other preposition in Spanish and in many other languages. See González (2021: 59–62).
17 Glosses not provided with sets of closely related examples under the assumption that coding with underlining, **bold**, and double underlining suffices.
18 As Lapesa (1983: 405) observed, *leísmo* is already present in *El cantar del mío Cid* (circa 1200).
19 I have read statements to this effect about Latin. I have not come across enough research on Greek to be able to attest to that statement for this language.
20 The frequency of *les* in (13) is lower than in (12). See answer to item # 25.
21 With the distinction between dialectal *leísmo* and general *leísmo* (González 2021, Chapter 3), counts of le/les for la/las/lo/los is an issue for further research. See also answer to 25 (page 30).
22 A search for the string "extraño mucho a" produced 19 results in Corpes XXI. None had Le(s). There was one sentence with *lo* duplicating the **verbed** (*Lo extraño mucho a Sebastián*). This is DO (**verbed**) "doubling" in River Plate Spanish. See Belloro (2015, Chapter 3) for DO doubling.

References

Aissen, Judith. 2003. Differential object marking: Iconicity vs. economy. *Natural Language and Linguistic Theory* 21. 435–483. www.jstor.org/stable/4048040

Alcina Franch, Juan & Blecua, José Manuel. 1975. *Gramática española*. Barcelona: Editorial Ariel. https://www.amazon.com/s?i=stripbooks&rh=p_27%3AJuan+Alcina+Franch&s=relevancerank&text=Juan+Alcina+Franch&ref=dp_byline_sr_book_1

Aranovich, Roberto. 2011. *Optional agreement and grammatical functions: A corpus study of dative clitic doubling in Spanish*. Pittsburgh: University of Pittsburgh. (Doctoral dissertation). http://d-scholarship.pitt.edu/6209/4/Optional_agreement_and_grammatical_functions.pdf

Belletti, Adriana & Rizzi, Luigi. 1988. Psych-verbs and Θ-theory. *Natural Language and Linguistic Theory* 6. 291–352. www.jstor.org/stable/4047649

Belloro, Valeria. 2007. *Spanish clitic doubling: A study of the syntax-pragmatics interface*. Buffalo, NY: State University of New York at Buffalo. (Doctoral dissertation). https://rrg.caset.buffalo.edu/rrg/Belloro-Spanish_Clitic_Doubling.pdf

Belloro, Valeria. 2015. *To the right of the verb: An investigation of clitic doubling and right dislocation in three Spanish dialects*. Cambridge, UK: Cambridge Scholars Publishing. www.cambridgescholars.com/resources/pdfs/978-1-4438-8039-8-sample.pdf

Bossong, Georg. 1991. Differential object marking in Romance and beyond. In Wanner, Dieter & Kibbee, Douglas A. (eds.), *New Analyses in Romance linguistics*, 143–170. Amsterdam/Philadelphia: Benjamins. https://benjamins.com/catalog/cilt.69

Bossong, Georg. 2021. DOM and linguistic typology: A personal view. In Kabatek, Johannes & Obrist, Philipp & Wall, Albert (eds.), *Differential object marking in Romance: The third wave*, 21–36. Berlin/Boston: De Gruyter. https://doi.org/10.1515/9783110716207

Bresnan, Joan. 1982. The passive in lexical theory. In Bresnan, Joan (ed.), *The mental representation of grammatical relations*, 3–86. Cambridge, MA: MIT Press. https://mitpress.mit.edu/9780262021586/

Company Company, Concepción. 2006. *Sintaxis histórica de la lengua española. Primera parte. La frase verbal.* Vol. 1. Ciudad de México: Universidad Nacional Autónoma de México/Fondo de Cultura Económica. www.fondodeculturaeconomica.com/Ficha/9786071620415/F

Cuervo, María Cristina. 2003. *Datives at large*. Cambridge, MA: MIT Press. (Doctoral dissertation). www.ai.mit.edu/projects/dm/theses/cuervo03.pdf

Cuervo, María Cristina. 2020. Datives as applicatives. In Pineda, Anna & Mateu, Jaume (eds.), *Dative constructions in Romance and beyond* (Open Generative Syntax 7), 1–39. Berlin: Language Science Press. https://langsci-press.org/catalog/book/258

Cuervo, Rufino José. [1847]1941. Notas a la gramática de la lengua castellana de D. Andrés Bello. In Bello, Andrés & Cuervo, Rufino José (eds.), *Gramática de la lengua castellana*. Buenos Aires: Librería Perlado.

Dryer, Matthew S. 1986. Primary objects, secondary objects, and antidative. *Language* 62(4). 808–845. www.jstor.org/stable/415173

Fábregas, Antonio. 2013. Differential object marking in Spanish: State of the art. *Borealis* 2(2). 1–80. http://dx.doi.org/10.7557/1.2.2.2603

Fernández-Ordóñez, Inés. 1999. Leísmo, laísmo y loísmo. In Bosque Muñoz, Ignacio & Demonte Barreto, Violeta (eds.), *Gramática descriptiva de la lengua española*, Vol. 1, 1317–1397. Madrid: Espasa Calpe. www.rae.es/obras-academicas/obras-linguisticas/gramatica-descriptiva-de-la-lengua-espanola

Fernández Ramírez, Salvador. 1987. *Gramática española. El pronombre*. 2nd ed. Vol. prepared by José Polo. Madrid: Arco/libros, S.A. ISBN: 84-7635-019-8

García, Erica C. 1975. *The role of theory in linguistic analysis: The Spanish pronoun system*. Amsterdam: North-Holland.

García-Miguel, José M. 2015. Variable coding and object alignment in Spanish: A corpus-based approach. *Folia Lingüística* 49. 205–256. https://doi.org/10.1515/flin-2015-0007

González, Luis H. 1997. *Transitivity and structural case marking in psych verbs: An HPSG fragment of a grammar of Spanish.* Davis, CA: University of California. (Doctoral dissertation). www.proquest.com/openview/4bba6135fcdbc9c5749d75be d674d68a/1?pq-origsite=gscholar&cbl=18750&diss=y

González, Luis H. 2021. *The fundamentally simple logic of language: Learning a second language with the tools of the native speaker.* London: Routledge. www.routledge.com/9780367688318

González, Luis H. 2022. *Understanding and teaching reflexive sentences in Spanish.* London: Routledge. www.routledge.com/9781032101873

Gutiérrez Ordóñez, Salvador. 1977–1978. Sobre los dativos "superfluos". *Archivum: Revista de la Facultad de Filología* 27–28. 415–452. https://reunido.uniovi.es/index.php/RFF

Gutiérrez Ordóñez, Salvador. 1999. Los dativos. In Bosque Muñoz, Ignacio & Demonte Barreto, Violeta (eds.), *Gramática descriptiva de la lengua española*, Vol. 2, 1855–1930. Madrid: Espasa Calpe. www.rae.es/obras-academicas/obras-linguisticas/gramatica-descriptiva-de-la-lengua-espanola

Keniston, Hayward. 1937. *The syntax of Castilian prose: The sixteenth century.* Chicago: The University of Chicago Press. http://onlinebooks.library.upenn.edu/webbin/book/lookupid?key=ha000908129

Laca, Brenda. 2006. El objeto directo. La marcación preposicional. In Company Company, Concepción (dir.), *Sintaxis histórica de la lengua española. Parte 1. La frase verbal*, 423–479. México, DF: Universidad Autónoma de México/Fondo de Cultura Económica. www.fondodeculturaeconomica.com/Ficha/9786071620415/F

Lapesa, Rafael. 1983. *Historia de la lengua española.* 9ª ed., corregida y aumentada. Madrid: Gredos. https://filologiaunlp.files.wordpress.com/2012/04/rafael-lapesa-historia-de-la-lengua-espanola.pdf

Levin, Beth. 1995. *English verb classes and alternations.* Chicago: The University of Chicago Press. https://press.uchicago.edu/ucp/books/book/chicago/E/bo3684144.html

Maldonado, Ricardo. [1999]2006. *A media voz. Problemas conceptuales del clítico se.* México, DF: Universidad Nacional Autónoma de México.

Marcos Marín, Francisco. 1978. *Estudios sobre el pronombre.* Madrid: Gredos. (PDF) Estudios sobre el pronombre | Francisco Marcos-Marín – Academia.edu.

Pylkkänen, Liina. 2008. *Introducing arguments.* Cambridge, MA: MIT Press. https://mitpress.mit.edu/9780262662093/introducing-arguments/

RAE (Real Academia Española). 1973. *Esbozo de una nueva gramática de la lengua española.* 21st reprinting. Madrid: Espasa Calpe, S.A.

RAE/ASALE (Real Academia Española y Asociación de Academias de la Lengua Española). 2009. *Nueva gramática de la lengua española. Sintaxis II.* Madrid: Espasa. www.rae.es/obras-academicas/gramatica/nueva-gramatica-morfologia-y-sintaxis

RAE/ASALE (Real Academia Española y Asociación de Academias de la Lengua Española). 2010. *Nueva gramática de la lengua española. Manual.* Bogotá: Editorial Planeta Colombiana S.A. www.rae.es/obras-academicas/gramatica/manual-de-la-nueva-gramatica

Snyder, William & Hyams, Nina. 2015. Minimality effects in children's passives. In di Domenico, Elisa & Hamann, Cornelia & Matteini, Simona (eds.), *Structures, strategies and beyond: Essays in honour of Adriana Belletti (Linguistik Aktuell/Linguistics Today, 223)*, 343–368. Amsterdam: John Benjamins. https://doi.org/10.1075/la.223

Vázquez Rozas, Victoria. 2006. Gustar-type verbs. In Clements, Joseph Clancy & Yoon, Jiyoung (eds.), *Functional approaches to Spanish syntax*, 80–114. New York: Palgrave Macmillan. https://pdfs.semanticscholar.org/49d3/117788a84917f086ae694f6ae482 ff075fce.pdf?_ga=2.201348755.369220713.1597701565-1866771009.1594303638

Wasow, Thomas. 1977. Transformations and the Lexicon. In Culicover, Peter & Wasow, Thomas & Akmejian, Adrian (eds.), *Formal syntax*, 327–360. New York: Academic Press. www.amazon.com/Formal-Syntax-Peter-W-Culicover/dp/0121992403

Wirnsberger, Markus. 2006. *El complemento indirecto y los dativos del castellano*. Manuscript. Berlin: Freie Universität Berlin. www.markus-wirnsberger.de. (Last accessed December 2021).

3 Against the need for 11 or more types of sentences with an indirect object in Spanish and in other languages

3.1 Eleven types of sentences with a dative (an indirect object) in Spanish

The following table shows 11 types of dative (indirect object) sentences in Spanish. This table was built with sentences (29) to (39) from MC Cuervo (2003: 29–30).– Similar tables were built from discussions on the indirect object (IO) for French, Latin, Polish, and Portuguese (Table 3.2 to Table 3.7). The reader will see that the participant "duplicated" with an IO (the participant double-underlined) *gets something or loses it. Or has it*. As Chapter 4 shows, that participant "stays" in the sentence when it is new information or when it is TOPICALIZED; that is, expressed in preverbal position.

If we ask speakers what happened to each of the participants in each of the following 11 sentences, they will not have much trouble in answering that question. They will say, for example, that now Gabi has a dictionary, we all have little sandwiches to eat with our tea, Andreína lost (does not have for now) the privilege to use her bicycle, Valeria has a car that is washed now, etc. Each of those IOs is a <u>benefactee</u> or a <u>malefactee</u>, and any speaker infers, without any conscious effort, that something good happened to Gabi, to Valeria, to Laura, and to us. Speakers also infer that something not good happened to Andreína and to Carolina. Every speaker knows that if *Pablo <u>le</u> rompió la radio <u>a Carolina</u>*, Pablo is the breaker, the radio is the broken, and Carolina is the <u>malefactee</u> because she "received" some harm from that breaking event. That sentence means that her radio is not working; therefore, Carolina does not have a radio that works, if that is the only radio she can use.

Contrary to Gabi, Valeria, Carolina, Laura, and we (us), nothing happened to Daniela. She simply lives in a world in which she does not have a *gusto* 'liking' for cats. The fact that *gustar* is a STATIVE verb predicts that state of affairs. A STATIVE verb expresses an interval during which a participant finds themselves, and that state lasts until a change causes the participant to exit it. *Appeal*(1), *belong*, *matter*, and *seem* are a few IO takers in English that happen to be stative verbs and that are used more often than not with two participants, a **verbed** and a <u>verbee</u>. If we sent Grandma our children, she enters

38 *Against the need for types of sentences with an indirect object*

Table 3.1 Types of sentences with an indirect object in Spanish. MC Cuervo's examples 29–39 (Cuervo 2003: 29–30)

1. Directional transitive activity verb (*a* 'to') → recipient	*Pablo le mandó* **un diccionario** *a Gabi*. Pablo.NOM her.DAT sent a dictionary to Gabi.DAT[1] 'Pablo sent <u>Gabi</u> **a dictionary**'. (Also: Pablo sent **a dictionary** <u>to Gabi</u>.)
2. Creation → benefactive	*Pablo nos preparó* **sandwichitos de miga** *a todos*. Pablo.NOM us.DAT fixed sandwiches small for all.DAT 'Pablo fixed <u>us all</u> **tea sandwiches**'. (Also: Pablo fixed **tea sandwiches** <u>for all of us</u>.)
3. Directional transitive activity verb (*a* 'from') → source	*Pablo le sacó* **la bicicleta** *a Andreína*. Pablo.NOM her.DAT took away the bicycle to Andreína.DAT 'Pablo took **the bicycle** from Andreína'. (Pablo took away the bicycle from Andreína)
4. Non-directional transitive activity verb → possessor	*Pablo le lavó **el auto** *a Valeria*. Pablo.NOM her.DAT washed the car.ACC to Valeria.DAT 'Pablo washed **Valeria's car**'. (Pablo washed **her car** <u>for Valeria</u>.)
5. Stative transitive verb → possessor	*Pablo le admira* **la paciencia/la campera** *a Valeria*. Pablo.NOM her.DAT admires the patience/the jacket.ACC to Valeria.DAT '<u>Pablo</u> admires **Valeria's patience/jacket**'.
6. Unergative (intransitive) verb → ethical dative (benefactive/ malefactive)	***Juanita*** *ya le camina (*a Vicky)*.[2] Juanita.NOM already her.DAT walk (Vicky.DAT) 'Juanita can already walk on her/Vicky'. *Mafalda no les toma* **la sopa** *a los padres*. 'Mafalda doesn't eat **the soup** on them/her parents'.
7. Unaccusative verb of change or movement → location/recipient	*A Gabi le llegaron* **dos cartas** *de Londres*. to Gabi.DAT her.DAT arrived two letters.NOM from London 'Gabi got two letters from London'. (Lit: '<u>to Gabi</u> arrived **two letters** from London'.)
8. Causative verb → affected	*Emilio le rompió* **la radio** *a Carolina*. Emilio.NOM her.DAT broke the radio.ACC to Carolina.DAT 'Emilio broke **the radio** on Carolina'.
9. Unaccusative psychological predicate → experiencer	*A Daniela no le gustan* **los gatos**. to Daniela.DAT not her.DAT like the cats.NOM 'Daniela doesn't like **cats**'.
10. Unaccusative existential verb → possessor	*A Laura le sobraron* **veinte pesos**. to Laura.DAT her.DAT were-extra twenty pesos 'Laura had **twenty pesos** left'. (Lit: To Laura were extra twenty pesos.)
11. Inchoative → affected	*A Carolina se le rompió* **la radio**. to Carolina.DAT se.REFL her.DAT broke the radio.ACC 'The radio broke on Carolina'. (Lit: To Carolina broke the radio.)

the state of having our children when they get to her house. She is in the state of having them until she exits that state by causing them to leave her house. Having our children is a state in which Grandma finds herself during the time our children are with her. With this short explanation, we can state that an IO means acquisition, possession, or loss of the **verbed**.

Thus, the meaning of each of those IOs is straightforward, regardless of the type of verb and putative semantic role for the IO in each sentence: each IO is a verbee. Interpretation is not a problem for any speaker; not even for those who do not know what IO, dative, or verbee is, and that is the overwhelming majority of speakers.

Do speakers need to learn each type of verb and each type of semantic role in Table 3.1 (and in Table 3.2 to Table 3.7)? Fortunately, no. Speakers understand and produce all types of sentences with an IO, but most speakers are not aware of any of the distinctions in those tables. Those categories are unnecessary, and some of them might not be correct. For example, most scholars will agree that the sentences with *send* in type (1), with *take away* in type (3), and with *wash* in type (4) express an ACCOMPLISHMENT or an ACHIEVEMENT, not an ACTIVITY.³ If Pablo made us little sandwiches, that means that he made **them** for us, gave **them** to us, and we have **them** now. To piggyback on an expression in English, we can have our little sandwiches and eat them, too. If Pablo washed Valeria's car, Valeria has a car that is clean now. She obviously owns her car, and that car is in a state of cleanliness right after Pablo washed it for her. If he admires her patience, Valeria has Pablo's admiration. At least for her patience. The fact that Pablo has admiration for her patience is an abstract possession but possession, nonetheless. If I tell the reader that *someone gave me **the finger** today*, every reader will infer that I received an insult today, which I own in an abstract way. No speaker of English is going to think that I had a finger transplant. Indeed, if I had a finger transplant, I would say that *someone gave me a finger today*. Interestingly, this mandatory IO in English uses the definite article as the determiner for *finger* and not the possessive adjective, as English does with many other **verbeds** whose determiner is a possessive adjective (*you have put on your fancy hat, she has washed her hair, I have not shaved my beard in three days*, etc.).

To summarize, understanding and producing the 11 types of sentences with an IO in MC Cuervo (2003: 29–30) is not a challenge for the regular speaker. I would like to propose that what the speaker is doing is understanding (or putting together) the meaning of each of those words in word (and constituent) orders allowed in the language.⁴ The speaker is simply putting together the meaning of each word in phrases, and those phrases are put together, in turn, in orders allowed by their language. Observe that HEAVINESS explains why the sentence in (12b) sounds more natural in Spanish than (12a). In fact, English does the same. Begahel (1909, quoted in Aranovich [Roberto] 2011: 132) observed that "syntactic constituents are linearly ordered in a way in which shorter constituents precede longer constituents". (Roberto Aranovich's wording).

(12) a. <u>Le</u>   mandé   **un hermoso ramo   de flores**   <u>a mi esposa</u>.
her.DAT sent-I.NOM a beautiful bouquet of flowers.ACC to my wife.DAT
'<u>I</u> sent **a beautiful bouquet of flowers** <u>to my wife</u>'.
b. <u>Le</u>   mandé   <u>a mi esposa</u>   **un hermoso ramo   de flores**.
her.DAT sent-I.NOM to my wife.DAT a beautiful bouquet of flowers. ACC
'<u>I</u> sent <u>my wife</u> **a beautiful bouquet of flowers**'.

If we ask a child who does not know how to read who/what is the subject, DO, and IO in the sentences in Table 3.1, that child will be at a loss to answer. Will that child be able to tell who is the <u>sender</u> and who is the <u>recipient</u>? Who is the <u>breaker</u> and who ended up with their **radio broken**; that is, who is the one breaking the radio and who is the person whose radio got broken? Probably. Depending on the child's age. Remarkably, that child does not even have to have started school. The <u>askee</u> has several clues. First, distinguishing <u>breaker</u> from **broken** is relatively easy. Many children start understanding and producing sentences in the passive voice at the age of three to four years. By five years of age, children "are able to comprehend short passive constructions" with "relative ease" (Armon-Lotem & Haman &...et al. 2016: 1).[5] Second, the <u>benefactee</u> or <u>malefactee</u> is neither the <u>verber</u> nor the **verbed**. Third, in many languages, the <u>verbee</u> is always marked with a preposition. Even when there is no preposition, speakers of languages with two objects also know intuitively that only one of them is the **verbed** (often the inanimate) and the other (often animate) is the only one that will require a preposition, if those two objects are "unshifted" (*I sent flowers* <u>to my wife</u> is "unshifted"). Any regular speaker of Spanish and English knows that in (12), **the bouquet of flowers** is the **sent** and that <u>my wife</u> received those flowers, both in (12a) and in (12b). Any speaker of English also knows that if there is a **verbed** in (12b), that **verbed** is the sent. <u>My wife</u> was the recipient of what was sent. People do not send their spouse to flowers. In fact, the likelihood of the PRIMARY object (<u>my wife</u> in 12b) being animate and the secondary object being inanimate (**a beautiful bouquet of flowers**) is close to 99% in English, and perhaps higher.[6]

Native speakers and second language learners of Spanish at the Intermediate Low to Intermediate High level in the ACTFL scale (A1.2 to B1.2 in the CEFR scale) do not have any difficulty in understanding that each of the referents of the <u>verbee</u> is a <u>benefactee</u> or a <u>malefactee</u>: Gabi has a dictionary and two letters, we have little sandwiches, Andreína lost the privilege of using her bike, Carolina has a broken radio, Daniela does not have a liking for cats, etc.[7]

Against the need for more sentences with an indirect object 41

3.2 The verbee in three-participant sentences and in two-participant sentences

3.2.1 Sentences with verber, verbed, and verbee

Here are a few observations about the 11 types of sentences in Table 3.1 above. These observations suggest that if speakers can track verber, **verbed**, and verbee, there is no need to know any types of verbs or semantic roles (affected, benefactive, experiencer, goal, recipient, source, etc.).

Sentences (1–6, 8, 11) have three participants. In seven out of eight sentences (1–6, 8) the order is verber, **verbed**, verbee. The order verber, verbee, **verbed** is possible. It is preferred when the **verbed** is HEAVIER than the verbee, as (12b) above shows, both in English and in Spanish. Sentence (12b) parallels dative (IO) shift in English with one difference: the marker *a* is kept in Spanish. Dative shift is not mentioned as often in Spanish as it is in English, perhaps because the marker *a* is not dropped. It is remarkable, though, that the order verber, verbee, **verbed** occurs close to 31% of the time during the 20th century (Company Company 2006: 515).[8] In fact, if in sentence (2) we omit the IO (a todos), the resulting sentence will be understood. In that case, the marker *nos* is the IO. In that case, it can be said that the order is verber, verbee, and **verbed**. As Chapter 4 shows, the pronoun alone is much more frequent than the pronoun + the IO. Thus, seven out of the 11 sentences in the types of dative sentences in Cuervo (2003: 29–30) have the order verber, **verbed**, verbee. The eighth sentence has the order verbee, verber, **verbed**. Sentence (11) is a TOPICALIZATION of the verbee, a common order for sentences with three participants, particularly when the verber has been replaced with an INTRANSITIVIZING pronoun, as González (2022, §2.3) explains sentences like those in (11).

3.2.2 Sentences with verber, [verbed], and verbee

Let us now interrupt the discussion of MC Cuervo's types of IOs to account for one of the types in Polish in Table 3.7 below. The reason for the interruption is that such a type of IO is common not only in Spanish but in many other languages, including English.

(13) a. <u>Ewa</u>   pomagała <u>tym ludziom</u>.
    Eve.NOM helped   these people.DAT
    '<u>Eve</u> helped <u>these people</u>'.

Ayudar 'help' has variable case marking in Spanish.[9] Some speakers use a DO pronoun with it, yet others use an IO pronoun with it. It appears to some speakers that *ayudar* 'help' takes verber and **verbed**, and the verbed is pronominalized with a DO pronoun. However, many more speakers pronominalize the single object as if it were an IO.[10] There is good evidence that the one receiving some help is the benefactee, not the **verbed**. First, since the subject passes the verber test, what these speakers seem to be doing is assuming that *ayudar* is a verb with three participants whose **verbed** undergoes indefinite object deletion, as with verbs like *creer* 'believe', *enseñar* 'teach', *mentir* 'lie', *perdonar* 'forgive', *escribir* 'write', etc., as discussed in González (2021, §5.3). Second, it appears that the intuition behind *ayudar* is that this verb means *darle* **ayuda** *a alguien* 'give **help** to someone', and that explains why the animate object is expressed as an IO. That intuition is on the right track. RAE (2022) defines *ayudar* 'help' as *prestar **cooperación*** 'lend **cooperation**'. Third, the test discussed in González (2021, §5.3) would give conflicting results with this verb, and that is the reason why it was not included there. With that test, we see this:

(14) *A Isabel*   *le/**la***   ayudó una actitud positiva.
     To Isabel.DAT her.DAT/her.ACC helped an   attitude positive.NOM
     'To Isabel, a positive attitude was helpful to her'.
     'A positive attitude helped Isabel'.

However, we have shown that when an ANIMATE object (roughly speaking, a human) is postverbal, that object is indirect if it can (and often must) be duplicated with an IO pronoun, as in (15a). On the other hand, that duplication with a direct object pronoun results in ungrammaticality, as in (15b):

(15) a. *Una actitud positiva*   *le*   ayudó *a Margarita*.
     an   attitude positive.NOM her.DAT helped to Margarita.DAT
     'A positive attitude helped Margarita'.
  b. *Una actitud positiva la   ayudó a Margarita.[11]
     an attitude positive her.ACC helped to Margarita.ACC

There is clear evidence that *ayudar* is 'give help' in German, and presumably in many other languages. The single object of *helfen* 'help' and *danke* 'thank' in German is an IO (Van Valin & LaPolla 1997: 356; González 2021: 43). If *help* is *give help*, and *danke* is *give thanks*, we have accounted for the IO marking of those and similar verbs without stipulating that those verbs must be lexically marked in the LEXICON (mental vocabulary) of the language. In English, *help* is often replaced with the expression *give someone a hand* . In Spanish, *you give **A hand** to someone* when *you* help them, but *you* give **THE hand** to someone when you greet them; that is, when you shake their hand.

If *ayudar* is *prestar **cooperación*** 'lend **cooperation**', then the animate object of *ayudar* (like *mentir* 'lie' and the verbs in (8a-p) in González (2021: 83–84) will be an IO, and the sentences with *le/les* should sound more natural than those with *la/las* or *lo/los*.[12] Furthermore, the sentences with *le/les* should be more frequent. I leave that issue for further exploration to those with a focus on corpus linguistics.

The following section returns to the discussion of MC Cuervo's types.

3.2.3 Sentences with *verbee* and verbed (verberless sentences)

Sentences (9–10) are verberless, as explained in §2.1. Interestingly, they have verbee, **verbed** in that order in the sentence. See González (2021, Chapter 5) for a more predictive explanation of the true *gustar* verbs in Spanish.[13] He "tests" sentences with 56 verbs that are potentially verberless (like *pertenecer* 'belong to'). Eight of those sentences are left there to "test" readers in recognizing true *belong* verbs (approximately 40) from transitive verbs (false *belong* verbs): *asustar* 'frighten', *cansar* 'tire', *fascinar* 'fascinate', *preocupar* 'worry', *sorprender* 'surprise', *causar* 'cause', *producir* 'produce', and *ocasionar* 'cause'.[14] The verbs *llegar* 'arrive', *nacer* 'be born', *salir* 'appear' (as in *a mole appeared to Rose*), *surgir* 'arise' (as in *a problem arose*), *temblar* 'shake' ('tremble') are also part of those 56 sentences in that list. These last four verbs are verbs of movement, plus *nacer*. Thus, if we take away the eight verbs that are not really verberless, *be born*, and these four verbs of movement, it appears that Spanish has approximately 40 verberless verbs.

The verbs of movement are special because they are not just these four verbs mentioned above. Readers familiar with French and Italian (and with other languages with a choice in auxiliary of the equivalent verbs for *have* and *be*) probably know about the verbs in *la maison d'être* or *la casa di essere* in teaching materials for those languages. That list typically includes some 15 verbs. *Naître* 'be born' and *mourir* 'die' are among them. The rest are clearly verbs of movement: *aller, arriver, descender, devenir, entrer, être, monter, passer, partir, rentrer, rester, retourner, revenir, sortir, tomber*. Readers can now see how *naître* and *mourir* are, in a sense, verbs of movement. They are the verbs of the ultimate arrival and departure.

These are, of course, not the only verbs that take *être* or *essere* 'be'. The list of *être/essere* takers is infinite. So is the list of *avoir/avere* 'have' takers. As proposed in González (2021, Chapter 2), a sentence has the auxiliary *avere* in Italian if there is a verber in the sentence, regardless of whether the sentence is intransitive or transitive. A sentence takes *essere* if there is no verber in the sentence. Remember that sentence (2) in Chapter 1 shows that the notion of subject hides the distinction between a verber and a **verbed** (Ángela studied, **taxes** increased). It turns out that with verbs of movement, an animate subject (a human, roughly speaking) can be the verber AND the **verbed**. Consider these sentences in English:

(16) a. Roberto moved **the chair**.
 b. **Roberto** moved.

It is uncontroversial that in (16a) Roberto is the mover and the chair is the **moved**. What is Roberto in (16b)? He is the mover and the **moved**. Think about the mail and the mail person. The mail is the arrived. The mail does not arrive on its own. It must be brought by a mail person. However, the mail person is the arriver and the **arrived**. The mail person is the one who arrived when she/he has arrived. Surprisingly, *move*, perhaps the prototypical verb of movement, seems to be missing from the *maison d'être/casa di essere* diagrams.[15] Consider now:

(17) a. Roberto went to the store.
    b. *Roberto fue a la tienda.* (17b is 17a, 17d is 17c, and 17f is 17e in Spanish)
    c. *Roberto went.
    d. *Roberto fue.*
    e. **Roberto** went away.
    f. ***Roberto** se fue*. (cf. **Roberto** se movió vs. ??Roberto movió.)[16]

With the proposal in González (2022, Chapter 4), the *se* in (17f) indicates that Roberto is the gone. That is uncontroversial because if *he went away, he is* (the) *gone*. Is he the goer as well? Yes, he is. He is the goer and the gone. English morphology supports this claim with the word *goner*. With many verbs of movement used with just one participant, the subject of a sentence is the **verbed** if that participant is inanimate. If that participant is animate and if it is the one doing the moving, that participant is the verber and the **verbed**. Consider these sentences from Italian, discussed in Van Valin & LaPolla (1997: 416; examples from Centineo (1986[1996]):

(18) a. *Luisa   ha corso.*   (Activity [Van Valin & LaPolla 1997: 416])
    Luisa.NOM has run
    'Luisa has run'.
    b. *Luisa   è corsa a casa.*   (Activity accomplishment [Van Valin & LaPolla 1997: 416])
    Luisa.NOM is run   to home
    '**Luisa** has run home'.

When *correre* 'run' is used as an activity, Luisa is the runner. She is doing some running. When an end point is added to the sentence (the accomplishment of reaching her house), Luisa is the runner and the run. In a clear sense, she has run herself home. She's gone home; that is, she has gone home and she is (gone) home.

The verb *escape* in English offers further evidence for the subject of many sentences being the verber and the **verbed**. Suppose there is news that a detained person escaped. That person would hardly be referred to as the detained person who escaped. That detainee who escaped is going to be referred to as the escapee.[17] That person is clearly the escaped, which is referred to as the escapee, as predicted by González's (2021: 31) rule of dative (IO) overriding of the accusative (DO), when the latter is animate (and there is no other IO in the sentence). Thus, the escapee is the escaped detainee. Is she/he also the escaper? Yes. One can set someone free, but in an event of escaping, the **escapee** (a false verbee) and the escaper is the same person (or animal).

Thus, the only participant (the subject) of a sentence with a verb of movement is the **verbed** if that participant is not doing the moving. If the **moved** participant is the one doing the moving as well, that participant is the verber and the **verbed**, a situation that occurs when the participant is animate. When there is another participant different from the **verbed** involved in an event of movement, that participant cannot be the verber. It must be a verbee. That is exactly what happens in sentences (6) and (7) from MC Cuervo (2003: 29–30), and presumably in countless other sentences in many languages.

This section helps readers understand that if a letter is the **arrived**, and that if a letter arrived for Gabi, then Gabi is the benefactee. **The letter** belongs to her. She is the belongee. By the same reasoning, if there is some money **left to someone** (i.e. the person has some extra money), the person to whom that money is left ("remained to") is the benefactee. Therefore, speakers of Spanish do say that *a Laura le* sobraron **20 dólares** (Laura has 20 dollars left. Or lit: to Laura, 20 dollars are left). Interestingly, this example might be easier for speakers of English to understand if we "flip" the verb.[18] *A Laura le faltan* **20 dólares** 'Laura is lacking 20 dollars', not the best sentence in English. However, the paraphrase *20 dollars are lacking to Laura* should now be clearer in English, even if this is not what a native speaker would really say. This author is not a native speaker of English but has the intuition that a native speaker will probably say that *Laura is 20 dollars short*. Twenty dollars is what is lacking, and they are lacking to Laura.[19]

This section has proposed that all of the types of IOs in MC Cuervo (2003: 29–30) are understood and produced by speakers because they are tracking verber, **verbed**, and verbee, and they do so without the need to invoke classes of verbs (other than verberless verbs) or different types of IOs, depending on their semantic role (affected, experiencer, goal, possessor, recipient, source, etc.).[20] Verber and **verbed** (and verbee) are needed to determine who does **what** (to whom) in a sentence. The same explanation used for verberless verbs (*belong, matter*, etc.) accounts for verbs of movement, which are clearly verberless with an inanimate **verbed** (as in *a letter* arrived *for Gabi from London*). The intuition of a verbee as a benefactee or malefactee also explains *help* and *thank* (and *believe, forgive, lie, read, write*, among many other verbs), verbs that often take a single object with an IO pronoun (or just the IO pronoun) in languages like German, Polish, Spanish, etc. **These three languages** *belong to three different families*.

Our discussion of the types of IOs in MC Cuervo (2003: 29–30) was interrupted because it missed an important IO: the one discussed in (13), which appears in the IOs in Polish below (type 60). The discussion of types of IOs in four other languages is going to show that an explanation based on verber, verbed, and verbee is simpler than the different types in MC Cuervo (2003: 29–30) and four other scholars who discuss similar types of IOs in French, Latin, Polish, and Portuguese (§3.3 to §3.6 below). The simplicity of the present proposal explains why regular speakers understand and produce sentences with an IO, without knowing types of verbs or the type of semantic role for a given IO. The preceding discussion explains all of them. Interestingly, other types are "named".

Readers can confirm in Tables 3.2 to 3.7 that the same explanation applies to most of those examples in those languages. As readers go through the following tables, they will be able to confirm that the IO (or the primary object) of sentences with three participants are all verbees. By virtue of being a benefactee or a malefactee, a verbee owns **something** (**something** belongs to them), obtained **it**, or lost **it**. Crucially, the benefactee or malefactee does not pass the **verbed** entailment, which the **verbed** does.

3.3 Types of sentences with a dative (an indirect object) in four other languages

3.3.1 Types of sentences with an indirect object in Latin (Van Hoecke 1996: 3–37)

Type (20) would be a case of general *leísmo* in Spanish, as proposed in González (2021: 31). MC Cuervo (2003: 29–30) was wise not to include an example like this one. But that shows that the categories might be arbitrary. Type (21) is more a locative than an IO. Scholars familiar with the IO know that the marker (*to* or *for* in English) of the IO in many languages comes from a preposition (or particle) whose original meaning was the expression of movement towards a destination or location.[21] Types (23) and (26) are both exemplified with sentences with the copula *be*, which takes a verbee (an IO) in many languages as well, and never allows an accusative (a DO). Positing two different types of IOs with the same verb is a red flag which suggests that the categories are difficult to keep apart. Even for scholars. One of the examples for type (22) has *his fellow citizens* marked as an IO in the fragment "to protect his fellow citizens". He is clearly the protector and his fellow citizens are the **protected**. This is a case similar to dialectal *leísmo* in Spanish (González 2021: 33–38, and references therein). Type (24) has again a "locative". However, this time the locative is inalienable possession (a part of the body). *What voice flew to my ears*. In Spanish, *cuál voz voló a mis oídos*, which most native speakers will render as ***cuál voz me voló a los oídos***, coding the possession with the IO *me* and changing the *MY* ears to *LOS oídos*. The *voz* 'voice' is

Table 3.2 Types of sentences with an indirect object in Latin

19.	Dativus proper	*Caesar* **regnum** *Cleopatrae* dedit.[22] Caesar.NOM kingdom.ACC Cleopatra.DAT gave 'Caesar gave **the kingdom** to Cleopatra'.
20.	Dativus commodi/ Incommode	*Fortuna* favet ***fortibus***. Fortune.NOM favors brave.DAT 'Fortune favors **the brave**'. (Notice that Van Hoecke marks *fortibus* as a verbee. This author marks it as a **verbed**.). Jessie Craft and Jeff Lerner (PC, 2022) have confirmed that *the brave* are *the **favored***.
21.	Dativus of approach	*Puer* adnatat *delphino*. Child.NOM approach by swimming dolphin.DAT 'The child swam to the dolphin'. (cf. Spanish: #El niño le acercó nadando **el niño** al delfín → **El niño** se le acercó nadando al delfín. Also: **El niño** se le acercó a nado al delfín.). See González (2022, Chapter 2) for an explanation of "IO" reflexivization.
22.	Dativus finalis	***Facundiam*** tuendis *civibus* exercebat. Eloquence.ACC protect.DAT-GER fellow citizens.DAT practiced 'He practiced **eloquence** to protect **his fellow citizens**'. (See in the explanation on page 46 why this author marks **his fellow citizens** as a **verbed**.)
23.	Dativus possessivus	*Amplissimae* *tibi* *divitiae* sunt. very great.NOM you.DAT riches.NOM are 'Very great riches are at your disposal'. 'You have very great riches'. (cf. English: **Great riches** belong to you. Lit: Grandes riquezas te son.)
24.	Dativus sympatheticus	*Nescio* *qua vox* **ad aures** *mihi* advolavit. not know-I.NOM what voice.NOM to ears.ACC me.DAT flew 'I do not know **what voice** flew to my ears'. (Lit: I do not know **what voice** to my ears me flew.) (Knower = I; known: **what voice flew to my ears**; flyer/flown: **what voice**; flyee = to my ears) *Dionysius* *sibi* adureba **capillum**. Dionysius.NOM himself.DAT had burnt hair.ACC 'Dionysius had his hair burnt'. (cf. Spanish: A Dionysius se le quemó **el pelo**.)
25.	Dativus auctoris	*Caesari* omnia erant agenda. Caesar.DAT everything.NOM were do.NOM-GER 'Everything had to be done by Caesar'. (cf. Spanish: A César le tocaba/le correspondía **hacer todo**.)
26.	Dativus iudicantis	*Quintia* formosa est *multis*. Quintia.NOM beautiful.NOM is many.DAT 'Quintia is beautiful in the eyes of many'. (cf. Spanish: *Quintia les es hermosa a muchos*. **Quintia** les parece hermosa a muchos. Quintia es hermosa para muchos.)
27.	Dativus ethicus	*Eg* **hanc machaeram** *mihi* consolari volo. I.NOM this sword.ACC me.DAT console-INF want-I 'I want to console this dear sword'.

uncontroversially **the flown**. *My ears* are the locative. But when a locative is animate, it appears that the IO (of benefit or harm) can prevail over a locative interpretation.

If a speaker of Spanish who does not know much Latin had to make sense of (25), that speaker would not have a very difficult task. I am that speaker who knows no Latin.[23] I would say that the meaning is *A César le tocaba* **hacer todo** (= *A César le correspondía* **hacer todo**). The sentence with *tocar* shows two *tocar* verbs in Spanish. *Tocar*(1) 'touch', with toucher and **touched**. *Tocar*(2); that is, to be one's turn (*tocarle el turno a uno*), with **touched** and touchee. It might be easier for speakers of English to see **the point** with *sound*(1): *They sounded* **the alarm** (sounder and **sounded**) vs. *sound*(2): *How does* ***a Frappuccino coffee*** *sound to you?* (**sounded** and soundee).

3.3.2 Types of sentences with an indirect object in Portuguese (de Andrade Berlinck 1996: 119–151)

Judging by the examples used, there is no discernible difference among type 28 (material transfer), type 30 (physical motion), type 31 (abstract motion), and, for that matter, type 29 (verbal and perceptual transfer). One of the examples for type 33 (transitive possessive dative [IO]) is the same as one for *dativus sympatheticus* in Latin. Type (34) has obeying *às regras de trânsito* marked as an IO. It makes much more sense to think that someone obeys **the rules** to a person/to an authority. In Spanish, it is common to say *obedecerle a alguien* 'obey someone **the rules**', 'obey **someone's rules**', or simply 'obey someone'. It is uncontroversial that the rules are the **obeyed** and the person/authority whose rules or commands one obeys is the obeyee. There are sentences with verberless verbs in type 34 (*belong, concern*), type 36 (*matter*), type 37 (*hurt*). There are sentences with verbs of movement in type 35 (*escape, come*), in type 37 (*tremble*), and in type 38 (*arrive*). In short, it appears that **this explanation of the types of IOs in Portuguese** might not be very helpful for learners of this language. On the other hand, with verber, **verbed**, and verbee, no learner (or scholar) of Portuguese will need to understand these types of IOs to understand the benefactee or malefactee in any sentence in the language.

The observation that scholars have marked DOs as if they were IOs (***fortibus*** in Latin [type 20], ***às regras de trânsito*** in Portuguese [type 34]) corroborates the claim in Chapter 2 that distinguishing DOs from IOs is extremely difficult, if we use subject, DO, and IO. With the **verbed** entailment, a **verbed** is more easily trackable, as children presumably do in close to all languages in the world when they unaccusativize (passivize) a **verbed** (*dinner was cooked*). Many children start to understand and produce sentences in the passive voice at the age of three to four years. By five years of age, children "are

Table 3.3 Types of sentences with an indirect object in Portuguese

TRANSITIVE	
28. Material transfer	Não entregaram **as mercadorias** <u>ao comprador</u>. not delivered-they.NOM the merchandise.ACC to the buyer.DAT[24] '<u>They</u> did not deliver **the merchandise** <u>to the buyer</u>'. <u>Maria</u> tomou-<u>lhes</u> **tudo que tinham**. Mary.NOM took them.DAT all that (they) had '<u>Maria</u> took **everything they had** from them'.
29. Verbal and perceptual transfer	Ela **me** ensinou a **técnica de leitura**. She.NOM me.DAT taught the technique of reading.ACC '<u>She</u> taught <u>me</u> **the reading technique**'.
30. Physical motion	No aniversário do amigo levou- **<u>lhe</u>** **um libro**. On birthday of-the friend took-he.NOM him.DAT a book.ACC 'On his friend's birthday, <u>he</u> took **him** **a book**'.
31. Abstract motion	**Os trabalhos** <u>lhe</u> foram submetidos ontem. The papers.NOM him.DAT were submitted yesterday '**The papers** were submitted <u>to him</u> yesterday'.
32. "Dativus commodi/ incommodi"	*Ele* abre a **porta** <u>aos convidados</u>. He.NOM opens the door for the guests '<u>He</u> opens **the door** <u>for his guests</u>'. <u>O rapaz</u> **lhe** pôs o **livro** na estante. the boy.NOM him.DAT put the book.ACC in-the bookcase '<u>The boy</u> put **the book** in the bookcase <u>for him</u>'.
33. The transitive possessive dative	*Eu* queimei-<u>lhe</u> **os cabelos**. I.NOM burned him/her.DAT the hair.ACC '<u>I</u> burned **her/his hair** <u>(for him/her)</u>'. <u>Maria</u> limpou-<u>me</u> **o casaco**. '<u>Mary</u> cleaned **my coat** <u>for me</u>'. <u>Eu</u> descasquei-<u>lhe</u> **a laranja**. '<u>I</u> peeled **his/her orange** <u>(for him/her)</u>'.
INTRANSITIVE	
34. Dative of interest	<u>João</u> sempre obedeceu às **regras de trânsito**. John.NOM always obeyed to the rules of traffic.DAT '<u>John</u> has always obeyed **the traffic laws**'. (See in the discussion why I marked **the traffic laws** as the verbed.) *O edifício* pertence <u>a um milionário de petróleo</u>. '**The building** belongs <u>to a petroleum millionaire</u>'. *O assunto* <u>lhe</u> concernia muito particularmente. '**The subject** concerned **him** quite specifically'.
35. Dative of motion	**Alguns erros de ortografia** <u>me</u> escaparam. Some errors of orthography.NOM me.DAT escaped '**Some orthographic errors** have escaped <u>my attention</u>'. (Lit: **some ortographic errors** escaped <u>me</u>'.) *Veio*-<u>lhe</u> **uma necessidade enorme de sair**. (it) came her/him.DAT a need enormous of leaving '<u>He</u> felt **a tremendous desire to go out**'. (Lit: It came <u>to her/him</u> **an enormous need to go out**.)

(*Continued*)

Table 3.3 (Continued)

36. Psychological movement	*A inteligência do rapaz agradou a todos.*[25] the inteligence of-the boy.NOM pleased (to) everybody.DAT 'The boy's intelligence pleased **everybody**'. *A eles não importa como você utiliza o seu tempo de trabalho.* to them.DAT not matter how you use the your time of work 'To them, it does not matter **how you make use of your working time**'.	
37. Intransitive possessive dative	*Dõem-me as costas.* aches-me.DAT the back.NOM **My back** aches (me). *Tremem-lhe as mãos.* tremble-her/him.DAT the hands.NOM 'Her/his hands are trembling'. (Lit: **the hands** tremble to her/him. From: something causes **the hands** to tremble to her/him.)	
38. Dativus ethicus	*Não me chegue tarde!* do not me.DAT arrive late 'Do not arrive late on me!' *Conta-me bem essa história ao rapaz!* tell-me.DAT well that story.ACC to-the boy.DAT 'Go and tell me **this story** well to the boy!' (Intended meaning: Go and tell on my behalf that story to the boy!). (cf. Spanish: ¡Cuéntamele bien **esa historia** al muchacho! Intended meaning: Go and tell the boy **that story** on my behalf! On my behalf = for my benefit. The intuition might be that the boy will be the one benefiting more from the story [he will learn an important lesson]. The me might be the possessive. It is my son.).[26]	

able to comprehend short passive constructions" with "relative ease" (Armon-Lotem & Haman &…et al. 2016: 1).[27]

3.3.3 Types of datives with an indirect object in French (Melis 1996: 40–51). Three-term constructions

Unlike de Andrade Berlinck (1996), Melis (1996) "merges" material transfer and notional transfer in type (40). The sentences in type (41) might be grouped together with those in type (40), except that this scholar (Melis) distinguishes between lexical attribute IOs and non-lexical ones. The difference is that the former are the so-called argumental IOs (verbs with verber, **verbed**, and verbee in its LEXICAL entry), whereas the latter are verbs without a verbee in its lexical entry. What happens is that a verbee can be added to sentences with these verbs. As §4.5 shows, a verbee can be added to many verbs, including the copula *be*. By the same token, a verb with a verbee in its lexical

Against the need for more sentences with an indirect object 51

Table 3.4 Types of sentences with an indirect object in French. Three-term constructions

39. Dative of equivalence	*Il lui préfere **Hélène**.* he.NOM him.DAT prefer Helen.ACC[28] 'He prefers **Helen** to him/her'.
40. Lexical attributive dative => transferencia física o nocional	*Les parents lui ont donné **trois livres**.* the parents.NOM him.DAT have given three books.ACC 'His parents gave him **three books**'. *Il lui présenta **le président**.* he.NOM him.DAT introduces the president.ACC 'He introduced **the president** to him'. *Je lui ai acheté **cette montre**.* I.NOM him.DAT have bought this watch.ACC 'I bought **this watch** from him'. *Pardonnez-nous **nos offenses**.* forgive-us.DAT our offenses.ACC 'Forgive us **our sins**'.
41. Non-lexical attributive dative => beneficiary, possessor	*Il lui a fermé **la porte**.* he.NOM him.DAT has closed the door.ACC 'He shut **the door** on him'. *Elle lui tricote **un pull**.* she.NOM him.DAT knits a sweater.ACC 'She is knitting **a sweater** for him'. *Les journaux lui fabriquent **un passé**.* the newspapers.NOM him.DAT fabricate a past.ACC 'The papers are fabricating **a past** for him'. *Il s'envoie **trois tasses de café** en un quart d'heure.* he.NOM se-REFL-drinks three cups of coffee in a quarter... 'He takes **three cups of coffee** in a quarter of an hour'. (cf. Spanish: Él le toma tres tazas de café a él → Él se toma tres tazas de café.) *Il lui a acheté **une montre** chez Cartier.* he.NOM him.DAT has bought a watch at Cartier 'He bought **a watch** for him at Cartier'.
42. Lexical partitive dative/ epistemic dative	*Elle te trouve **le nez** bien fait.* she.NOM you.DAT finds the nose.ACC well made 'She thinks **that you have a nice nose**'. (Lit: She finds a nice nose to you. She thinks that your nose is nice.)
43. Non-lexical partitive dative. Inalienable (and alienable!) possessor.	*Maman lui a lavé **les cheveux**.* mother.NOM him.DAT has washed the hair.ACC 'Mother washed **his hair**'. (Lit: Mom has washed him the hair.) *Il lui cire **les bottes**.* he.NOM him.DAT polishes the boots.ACC 'He polishes **his boots**'. (Lit: He polishes the boots for him.) *Une idée étrange lui traverse l'esprit.* a strange idea.NOM him.DAT traverses the spirit.ACC 'A strange idea crosses **his mind**'. (Lit: 'A strange idea crosses **the mind** to him')

(Continued)

Table 3.4 (Continued)

	*Il se peint **la main**.* he.NOM se-REFL paints the hand.ACC '<u>He</u> is painting his hand'. (cf. *Il peint sa main* . 'He represents his hand in a painting'. LM) *Il te glissa **un mot** à l'oreille.* he.NOM te.DAT drops a word.ACC to the-ear.DAT '<u>He</u> dropped **a word** in your ear'. (Lit: <u>He</u> glides **a word** <u>to your ear</u>. LHG)

entry (verbs of transfer, of communication, etc.) can be used in sentences without a <u>verbee</u>. And even without a **verbed**, as the question and answer in MC Cuervo (2010: 172) show: *–¿Vas a donar este año? – No, yo ya di.* ('– Are you going to donate this year? – No. I have already given'.). Unless you are a linguist, you probably do not know anything about this argumental/non-argumental distinction. Interestingly, you can understand the meaning of these sentences and the contribution of the <u>benefactee/malefactee</u> to their meaning, even if your knowledge of French is limited to understanding as best you can the sentences in French through the glosses offered.

This is the fourth language we have encountered, and here there is a new category: IO of equivalence (type 39). That might be acceptable if there were a good amount of overlap among the types in the four languages. There is not such a desirable overlap. A sign that each type is not what linguists call a NATURAL CLASS. A natural class is a set of linguistic items that follows a rule or a set of rules. Stop phonemes (/p/, /t/, /k/, /b/, /d/, /g/) are a natural class. Verberless verbs are a natural class. They can be shown to behave the same way when a rule is applied to them. One participant is the **verbed** and the other (usually the animate one) is the <u>verbee</u>: *appeal*(1), *appear, be, belong, cost, happen, matter, occur, remain, sound*(1).

Readers can see that the sentences that exemplify type (41) are what can be called a mixed bag. There is one sentence expressing physical creation (knitting **a sweater** <u>for someone</u>) and one expressing abstract (notional) creation (a newspaper fabricating **a past** <u>for someone</u>). <u>Someone</u> is buying **a watch** at Cartier <u>for someone else</u>. <u>Someone</u> is drinking **three cups of coffee** "<u>to himself</u>" in a quarter of an hour. These sentences are some of a few more in this category. There is not much to connect them. Except, of course, that there is a <u>benefactee</u> (or a <u>malefactee</u>) that would not pass the **verbed** entailment. That is the connection that speakers make. That is the piece of meaning that speakers track.

An example with *arrive*, a verb of movement, is found in two different types (45, 46). Type (45) has a mix of types. Verbs of movement (*arrive* and *go*) and some of the verberless verbs (*manquer* 'be lacking to' and *belong*). Verbs of movement and verberless verbs belong to a natural class under the assumption that there is a <u>verbee</u>, plus a **verbed**, which, if animate, can be THE **VERBED** AND THE <u>VERBER</u> with verbs of movement, as explained

Table 3.5 Types of sentences with an indirect object in French (Melis 1996: 51–57). Two-term constructions

44. Datives of equivalence	*Marie te resemble.* Mary te.DAT resemble.
45. Lexical attributive datives	*Il m'arrive* **une nouvelle aventure**. it.NOM m-arrive.DAT a new adventure.NOM '**A new adventure** is arriving for me'. *Le bleu lui va très bien.* le bleu.NOM her.DAT goes very well '**Blue** goes well on her'. (cf. Spanish: *El azul le va/viene muy bien.*) *Ce livre lui manque.* this book.NOM him.DAT lacks 'He misses this book'. (The meaning is probably 'This book is missing to him'). *Cette decision lui appartient.* this decision.NOM him.DAT belongs '**This decision** belongs to him'. *Il lui ment.*[29] he.NOM him.DAT lies 'He is lying to him'. *Il lui est fidèle.* he.NOM him.DAT is faithful 'He is faithful to him'.
46. Non-lexical attributive datives	*Il lui est né* **une fille**. it.NOM him.DAT is born a daughter.NOM '**A daughter** is born to him'. *Il m'est arrivé* **un etrange colis**. it.NOM me-DAT-has arrived a strange package '**A strange package** has arrived for me'.
47. Lexical partitive datives	*Ce trait lui est propre.* this characteristic.NOM him.DAT is peculiar 'This characteristic is peculiar to him'. *L'évidence m'est tombée dessus.* the evidence me.DAT-is dropped suddenly 'It suddenly became evident to me'.
48. Non-lexical partitive datives	*La tête lui tourne.* the head.NOM him.DAT turns 'His head is spinning'. (Lit: **His head** spins to him.) *Les larmes lui montaient aux yeux.* the tears.NOM him.DAT came to-the eyes.DAT 'Tears welled up in his eyes'. *Une idée lui passa par la tête.* an idea.NOM him.DAT passes by the head 'An idea crosses **his mind**'. (Lit: **An idea** passes/comes to his mind)

in §3.2.4 above. Type (45) has *be* also, which is also found in type (50) below, although in a somewhat different environment (as the controller of an infinitive). Native speakers can understand the meaning of a sentence (and produce similar sentences) expressing that someone is advising someone **(to**

Table 3.6 Types of sentences with an indirect object in French (Melis 1996: 57–59). Extensions of the attributive dative

49. The dative as the controller of an infinitive	*Je lui conseillai **de partir**.* I.NOM him.DAT advised of leaving 'I advised him **to leave**'. ***Partir me plaît.*** leaving.NOM me.DAT pleases 'I would like to leave'. (Lit: **Leaving** is pleasing to me.)
50. These two are special cases of the dative as the controller of an infinitive	*Il m'est difficile **de venir**.* it.NOM me.DAT-is difficult of coming 'It is difficult for me to come'. *Il lui appartient **de prender la décision**.* He.NOM him.DAT belong of making the decision 'He must make the decision'. (Spanish: *le compete* **tomar la decisión**; *le pertenece* **tomar la decisión**.) *Tu lui as fait/laisse/vu **manger le gâteau**.* you.NOM him.DAT has made/let/seen eat the cake 'You have made/let/seen him **eat the cake**'.
51. The peripheral dative	*Ça lui semblait/paraissait intéressant.* it.NOM him.DAT seem/appear interesting 'It seemed/appeared interesting to him'. *Tu vas me lui presenter **des excuses**!* you.NOM go me.DAT him.DAT ask (for) of-the excuses 'You should apologize to him'. (cf. Spanish: ([Tú] Vas y me le pides **excusas**. That is, you do me the **courtesy** of apologizing to him.)

do) something, without knowing the concept "controller of an infinitive". Lastly, type (45) also has *mentir* 'lie'. *Lie* is, in fact, a "lexical dative" (an IO-taking verb) because there is a lier, **the lie told**, and a liee. It should be in type 40 (notional transfer). The point here is that the types are not lacking in mismatches. Natural classes of linguistic items do not match and mix as freely as the types of IOs in this table. As presented in Table 3.1 to Table 3.7, *the types of sentences with an IO pronoun are not helpful for learners of any of those languages represented.*

3.3.4   Types of sentences with an indirect object in Polish (Rudzka-Ostyn 1996: 341–394)

The next section will offer some observations about the types of sentences with an IO in Polish. A connection among three languages is the reason for giving it a separate section. That connection might include many other languages. This is an invitation for scholars from other languages to explore further the explanation proposed in this section. Readers will remember that type (58) was discussed with the types of datives in Spanish proposed in MC Cuervo (§3.2.3).

Against the need for more sentences with an indirect object   55

Table 3.7 Types of sentences with an indirect object in Polish

NON-REFLEXIVE DATIVES	
52. Physical transfer => recipient	*Jan dał jej książkę.* john.NOM gave her.DAT book.ACC[30] 'John gave her a book'.
53. Dative of creation => recipient	*Kowalski wystawił synowi piękny dom.* mr. Kowalski.NOM built son.DAT beautiful house.ACC 'Mr. Kowalski built his son a beautiful house'.
54. Cognitive endpoint => recipient	*Pokazał dzieciom zabawki.* showed-he.NOM children.DAT toys.ACC 'He showed the children the toys'.
55. Non-volitional dative	*Ortografia sprawia Jankowi dużo kłopotu.* orthography.NOM causes John.DAT much trouble.ACC 'Orthography causes Johnny a lot of trouble'.
56. Non-human datives	*Poświęciłam czas pracy/studiom literackim.* devoted-I.NOM time work.DAT/literary studies.DAT 'I devoted my time to work/to literary studies'.
57. "Malefactive" dative	*Lokatorzy poniszczyli nam meble.* tenants.NOM damaged us.DAT furniture.ACC 'Tenants damaged our furniture'. (cf. Spanish: Los inquilinos nos dañaron los muebles.)
58. Quasi transitive dative => recipient	*Ewa pomagała tym ludziom.* eve.NOM helped these people.DAT 'Eve helped this people'. *Marysia im gotuje, pierze i sprząta.* mary.NOM them.DAT cooks launders and cleans 'Mary cooks for them and does their laundry and cleaning'. (cf. Spanish: Mary les cocina, les lava y les limpia.)
59. Impersonal dative => experiencer	*Słabo mi się robi.* faint (on) me.DAT się.REFL gets/becomes it 'I feel faint (on me)'. (cf. Spanish: (Se) me viene un desmayo = (Yo) me desmayo. Me estoy desmayando.) *Alez mi się chce jesc/pic/spac!* how me.DAT się.REFL wants-it.NOM eat/drink/sleep 'My, how hungry/thirsty/sleepy I am'. (I really feel like eating/drinking/sleeping.) (cf. Spanish: Se me antoja comer/beber/dormir. Also: (Yo) me muero de ganas de comer/beber/dormir.). *Ganas* 'desires'
REFLEXIVE DATIVES	
60. Non-reciprocal *sobie*	*Przyniósł sobie skrzynkę piwa.* brought-he.NOM self.DAT crate.ACC beer-GEN 'He brought himself a crate of beer'. *Uszyłam sobie sukienkę.* sewed-I.NOM self.DAT dress.ACC 'I made myself a dress'. (cf. Spanish: (Yo) Me hice un vestido. From: #Yo le hice un vestido a yo.)

(Continued)

Table 3.7 (Continued)

61. Reciprocal *sobie*	<u>Ministrowie</u> przekazali <u>sobie</u> **potrzebne dokumenty**. ministers.NOM transmitted self.DAT necessary documents.ACC '<u>The ministers</u> transmitted <u>to each other</u> **the necessary documents**'. (cf. Spanish: <u>Los ministros</u> <u>se</u> transmitieron **los documentos necesarios** unos a otros. From: #<u>los ministros</u> <u>les</u> transmitieron **los documentos necesarios** <u>a los ministros</u>.)
62. Prepositional dative	<u>Droga</u> wiodła <u>ku</u> <u>wsi</u>. road.NOM led to(wards) village.DAT '<u>The road</u> led to the city'. (cf. Spanish: <u>La carretera</u> llevaba [la gente] a la ciudad.)

3.4 Connecting <u>verber</u>, verbed, and <u>verbee</u> in Polish, in Italian, and in other languages

Let us begin with an IO reflexive in Polish, as glossed in Rudzka-Ostyn (1996: 370).

(63) a. *Uszyłam sobie sukienkę.*
   Sewed(I).NOM self.DAT dress.ACC
   'I dressed myself'. (Gloss by Rudzka-Ostyn).
   'I sewed myself a dress'. (Gloss by this author).

Observe that in this gloss the reflexive pronoun is marked as an IO, according to the almost universal assumption that an IO that is identical to the subject must be replaced with its corresponding reflexive pronoun. González (2021, Chapter 2) shows that a reflexive pronoun does not replace an IO that is identical to the subject. If that were the case, sentence (64a) and sentence (64b) in this example in Italian should be as indicated below. Strikethrough indicates the participant that is presumably replaced with the reflexive pronoun *si*.

(64) a. #<u>Francesca</u> gli ha tagliato **un dito** <s>a Francesca</s>.
       Francesca.NOM her.DAT has cut a finger.ACC to Francesca.DAT
       'Francesca has cut herself a finger'.
    b. *<u>Francesca</u> <u>si</u> ha tagliato **un dito**.

The problem is that (64b) is not a sentence in Italian, although it should be, because there is apparently a subject in the sentence (*Francesca*), and there is also a DO (*un dito*). This would make that sentence transitive. By a rule in Italian grammar that transitive sentences take the auxiliary *avere*, (64b) should be a sentence in Italian. It is not. That is a serious problem for an analysis of reflexivization based on the replacement of an IO with the corresponding reflexive pronoun when it is identical to the subject. It is also a problem for a grammar based on subject, DO, and IO.

Against the need for more sentences with an indirect object 57

González (2022, Chapter 2) offers ample evidence that a reflexive pronoun does not replace a DO or an IO when identical to the subject. A reflexive pronoun replaces the <u>verber</u> in the 15 or so types of reflexive sentences in Spanish. The same analysis can be applied to at least two dozen languages (González 2022, Chapter 5). Thus, if we apply a rule of <u>verber</u> replacement with a reflexive pronoun in Italian to (65a), we should get (65b). Strikethrough indicates the omitted <u>verber</u>, and *si* with single underline indicates that *si* is replacing the <u>verber</u>:

(65) a. *~~Francesca~~ <u>gli</u> ha tagliato **un dito** *a Francesca*.
       Francesca-NOM her.DAT has cut   a   finger to Francesca
   b. *<u>Francesca</u> <u>si</u> è tagliata* **un dito**. (TOPICALIZATION of the <u>verbee</u>)
      '<u>Francesca</u> has cut <u>herself</u> **a finger**'.

Remember that TOPICALIZATION is the expression of the <u>verbee</u> (or the **verbed**) in preverbal position. If the rule of auxiliary selection were a rule that "sees" a subject (nominative) and a DO (accusative), (64b) should be a sentence in Italian. It is not. If the rule at work is a rule that requires *avere* when there is a <u>verber</u> in the sentence, but that requires *essere* when there is no <u>verber</u> (as proposed in González 2021: 21), then (65b) should be a sentence in Italian. It is. With a nice bonus. With the auxiliary *essere*, the past participle and the **verbed** (or the <u>verbee</u>, if the <u>verbee</u> is the one promoted to preverbal position, as in 65b) agree. That rule of agreement applies to other languages that do not have a choice in auxiliary, but that use the equivalent of *be* for other functions. Spanish is one of those languages. It uses *ser* 'be' to express a sentence in the passive voice (*la puerta fue abierta* 'the door was opened') and *estar* 'be' to express a resultant state (*la puerta está abierta* 'the door is open').

Rules of language referring to subject, DO, and IO, predict that (64b) is a sentence in Italian. It is not. Rules of language referring to <u>verber</u>, **verbed**, and <u>verbee</u> predict that (65b) is a sentence in Italian. It is. With <u>verber</u>, **verbed**, and <u>verbee</u>, native speakers and L2 learners of Italian can choose correctly the auxiliary *avere* or *essere* if they can distinguish <u>verber</u> from **verbed**. They can do so because learners understand that if *Dad cooked dinner*, *Dad was the cook(er)*, and *dinner was cooked*. No speaker of any language understands that if *Dad cooked dinner*, #*Dad was the cooked*, and #*dinner was the cooker*. The same way that learners of Spanish (and many other languages) understand and produce at least ten types of sentences with a "reflexive" pronoun, without knowing that there are different names for those types of sentences, as explained in González (2022), learners of many languages understand and produce at least 11 types of sentences with an IO and without knowing that there are different names for those types of sentences, as explained in this chapter. The types of sentences with an IO are easily closer to 15 than to ten, if one wanted to really bring together the names in some of the languages that have close to that many types of sentences. That is an unnecessary exercise because this chapter has shown plenty of evidence that what speakers are doing is tracking <u>verber</u>, **verbed**, and <u>verbee</u>. Exploring further this proposal would be a smarter exercise. This is an invitation for scholars to expand this proposal to other languages and add to the evidence that rules of language are easier to state, understand, apply, and remember if they are formulated in terms of <u>verber</u>, **verbed**, and <u>verbee</u>.

3.5 In the classroom

One undergraduate student at the university where this author teaches was invited to write an honor thesis. She wanted to explore IOs. She had already written a class paper on the topic. With <u>verber</u>, **verbed**, and <u>verbee</u>, she was able to understand enough of MC Cuervo's doctoral dissertation (MC Cuervo 2003) to write in Spanish why the types of sentences with an IO in that dissertation are not really needed if one understands the two simple entailments that distinguish <u>verber</u> from **verbed** and can track <u>verber</u>, **verbed**, and <u>verbee</u> in all the examples of the 11 types. It is hard to see how a student will not get lost trying to follow that dissertation using subject, DO, and IO. I had the intuition that with her understanding of <u>verber</u>, **verbed**, and <u>verbee</u>, she would be able to understand at least 70% of MC Cuervo's dissertation. We cannot really measure her understanding. However, she was able to explain MC Cuervo's 11 types of sentences to attendees looking at a poster she prepared for an undergraduate research fair. She was also able to explain the 11 types at a conference on Spanish linguistics at The University of North Carolina at Chapel Hill in February of 2019.

As part of her honor thesis, we built the table in 3.1. Then, we color-coded it, following a textbook for Spanish, which does that (Whitley & González 2016). That color-coded table seems to help undergraduate students who come to my office when they want to understand IOs better or want to distinguish better DOs from IOs. In fact, the table is a great tool to introduce and give examples of <u>verber</u>, **verbed**, and <u>verbee</u>, from concrete ones to abstract ones.

Teachers from other languages with similar types of sentences with an IO can see how color-coding <u>verber</u>, **verbed**, and <u>verbee</u> can help students understand those sentences, without the need to understand and learn the types of verbs or types of semantic roles in those explanations. Tables like those in this chapter are used in classes of Spanish as an L2 with undergraduate students at the Intermediate Low to Intermediate High level in the ACTFL scale (A1.2 to B1.2 in the CERF scale).[31] They are also used in a graduate class for L2 learners of Spanish. This author teaches two such classes.

Teachers familiar with this book can now compile a table for their language that might be an improvement over the one(s) discussed here. Teachers of some languages might have to start almost from scratch. There are, however, plenty of examples here to guide them. It is conceivable that they will

Against the need for more sentences with an indirect object 59

see how they can bring together sentences that are presented in different parts of the textbook(s) they use. The table need not include the types of verbs and types of semantic roles, but rather concentrate on helping learners see how they can track verber, **verbed**, and verbee in an array of sentences using an IO.

Teachers and scholars who write L2 materials will also realize that verbs like *aburrir* 'bore', *asustar* 'frighten', *molestar* 'bother', *preocupar* 'worry', *sorprender* 'surprise', etc., must not appear on lists of truly *gustar* verbs like *costar* 'cost', *doler* 'hurt', *faltar* 'be lacking to', *importar* 'matter', *ocurrir* 'occur', *pertenecer* 'belong', *sobrar* 'have left', etc. Textbooks for Spanish will do a better job if they introduce *gustar* verbs comparing them to *belong, matter, seem*, etc. *Gustar* and those verbs are special because they are verberless. Teachers who read for the first time about verberless verbs might think that this explanation is too abstract or too difficult to be used in the classroom. It looks harder than it is because it is NEW. After all, remember that we have been learning languages with subject, DO, and IO for over 21 centuries. Verber, **verbed**, and verbee have been tested in the classroom for close to 30 years in classes from Spanish 1 in college to a graduate class on Spanish/English contrasts.

Let me finish this section with an anecdote and an answer to two questions. The anecdote answers one of two question that many teachers might ask. The first question is: Do students understand verber and **verbed**? They do. The student in the following anecdote was an undergraduate in her third year. Her major was Spanish. She was not even a minor in linguistics. In February of 2017, six of my undergraduate students were presenting at a conference at North Carolina State University in Raleigh, North Carolina, USA. One of the students was arguing precisely against the need for types of sentences with an IO. The organizer of the conference asked her, "where do verber, **verbed**, and verbee come from?" She replied, "I have been studying Spanish since Kindergarten. When I took a Spanish grammar class with Professor González, and he explained grammar using verber, **verbed**, and verbee, grammar made sense for the first time". The second question, which several students have asked, is the following: "why has nobody explained grammar to me with verber, **verbed**, and verbee?" The answer is simple: This is a new idea. I have been testing it in my teaching for about 30 years. But that research began being published in February 2021, only two years before this book was accepted for publication. At least five acquisition editors had rejected (or completely ignored) a book proposal with the theory of verber and **verbed**. One journal rejected at least four attempts to publish articles on verber and **verbed**. Samantha Vale-Noya and her team were the first publisher to accept my (single author) books. This is my fifth book published with Routledge. ¡*Un millón de gracias, Sam and Tassia Team*!

3.6 Conclusions

This chapter shows that the 11 or so types of sentences with an IO in many languages, which can be traced back to Latin and Greek, are not necessary to understand what those sentences express. A review of the sentences with an IO in MC Cuervo (2003: 29–30) shows that the IO in each type of sentence is a <u>benefactee</u> or a <u>malefactee</u> (a <u>verbee</u>). No speaker needs to be aware of the distinctions that "different" roles (affected, experiencer, goal, possessor, recipient, source, etc.) or different types of verbs express, whether in MC Cuervo (2003) or in RAE/ASALE 2010: 678–684 (transfer, communication, happening, pertinence, belonging, utility, necessity, sufficiency, etc.). Speakers understand that a true IO (as distinguished in Chapter 2 from DOs that at times take an IO pronoun) expresses the participant who gets something (<u>they</u> sent <u>you</u> **this book**), loses it (*a Andreína* <u>le</u> *quitaron* **la bicicleta** 'they took away Andreína's bike'), or owns it (**the bike** belongs <u>to Andreína</u>). The IO is a <u>benefactee</u> or a <u>malefactee</u> both in sentences with three participants and in verberless sentences (**integrity** matters <u>to good citizens</u>).

It would be reasonable to accept that different languages differ slightly on the types. One language might have a few transitive verbs (verbs with <u>verber</u> and **verbed**) rather than verberless verbs (verbs with <u>verbee</u>/**verbed**). English, not a robust <u>indirect-object</u> user, is such a language. The verb *like*, among a few other verbs, used to take subject and indirect object (*it liketh me*), as Whitley (2002: 145) observes. However, when different types of verbs are grouped in one type of sentence with an IO in a language (Type 41 in Melis 1996, discussed above) or the same verb appears in different types of sentences with an IO (*be* in Type 45 and Type 50 in Melis 1996, discussed above), one must admit that the types are not as well understood as they should be. On the other hand, regular speakers who do not know what a semantic role is can understand and produce sentences with a <u>verbee</u>, even when the <u>verber</u> or the **verbed** is not explicitly expressed in those sentences. The evidence shown in this chapter indicates that speakers do so because they are tracking <u>verber</u>, **verbed**, and <u>verbee</u>. Remarkably, L2 learners can do the same, although they do so after several explanations during several levels of an L2 and after lots of practice, as almost any L2 teacher can attest. The <u>verber</u>/**verbed** and <u>verbee</u>/**verbed** explanation proposed in this book will make that task easier for teachers to explain and for learners to understand and use in their L2 or n language.[32]

Notes

1 Abbreviations used: ACC(usative), DAT(ive), INF(initive), GER(und), NOM(inative), REFL(exive).
2 An asterisk (*) before a sentence means that native speakers rarely or never produce that sentence (or phrase). MC Cuervo marks this sentence as ungrammatical when *a Vicky* is added. A Google search in November 2022 for "*le camina a*" returned 4,390 results. Two of those results are:

(i) *Una cucaracha <u>le</u> camina <u>a la cantante Yuri</u> en pleno concierto.*
(ii) *¿Humberto de la Calle no <u>le</u> camina <u>a la paz total</u>?*

3 See Vendler (1967) for Aktionsart classes of verbs. Verbs like *run, sneeze, snore, walk* express activities. *Write* **a book**, *memorize* **a poem**, *sing* **a song** are accomplishments. Pop **a balloon**, break **your glasses**, find **your keys** are achievements.
4 I had written before that speakers put sentences together in a way reminiscent of what is intuitively understood as Frege's compositionality principle. It turns out that the compositionality principle is highly disputed. Beginning with the observation that Frege never formulated it, at least explicitly. See Pelletier (1994) for some discussion and further references.
5 This article was written by 19 contributors. See references for the full list.
6 The distinction between PRIMARY object and SECONDARY object was proposed in Dryer (1986: 814) for English and for many other languages. The primary object is the benefactee/malefactee (often animate), and it follows the verb without a preposition. The secondary object is the DO (often inanimate), and it follows the primary object. This distinction has been widely adopted. The distinction between **verbed** and verbee provides new arguments against that proposal. Further discussion of Dryer's proposal does not belong in this book.
7 www.actfl.org/sites/default/files/reports/Assigning_CEFR_Ratings_To_ACTFL_ Assessments.pdf
8 This frequency is when both objects are "fully" expressed; that is, not replaced with their corresponding pronoun. The IO pronoun might be in the sentence. Chapter 4 explains when it is expressed in the sentence (1) the IO pronoun alone, or (2) the IO + the IO pronoun, or (3) the IO only.
9 This short section (3.2.3) is taken almost word by word (including sentences 14 and 15) from González (2021: 87–88).
10 A simple Google search returned the following results (May 2020):

   (i) "*la ayudan*" = 220,000 (7.1%)
   (ii) "*lo ayudan*" = 738,000 (23.8%)
   (iii) "*le ayudan*" = 2,140,000 (69.01%)

11 Speakers of Spanish of the River Plate region (Argentina) might say sentences like this one. Most speakers of Spanish do not double a **verbed** that is in postverbal position. Belloro (2015: 39) discusses "Accusative doubling in Buenos Aires Spanish", perhaps because she was using a corpus of Buenos Aires Spanish. It is conceivable that the same phenomenon occurs in Uruguay as well. At least in the region closer to the River Plate Basin.
12 These are some of those sentences:

   (i) *El niño le habló [palabras] al papá.*
     'The child spoke [**words**] to his father'.
   (ii) *Los niños le leyeron [un cuento] a la mamá.*
     'The children read Mom [**a short story**]'.
   (iii) *El acusado le mintió al juez.*
     'The accused lied to the judge'. (cf. The accused told lies to the judge.)
   (iv) *El estudiante le obedeció [las órdenes] a la profesora.*
     'The student obeyed the professor [**her orders**]'.

13 The true *gustar* verbs (that can easily take two participants) in English are *appear, appeal*(1), *be, belong, cost, happen, matter, occur, seem, remain, sound*(1). There are other verberless verbs that are usually used with one participant: *die, exist, fall*, etc.
14 As in *A Rosa le ocasionó* **disgusto** *la noticia* 'the news caused/produced **disgust** in Rosa'. (cf. The news was disgusting to Rosa.)
15 I found the equivalent of *run* in two out of five of those diagrams. The Italian verb *andare* 'walk' was also occasionally found. The 15 or so verbs of movement are probably the most frequent verbs of movement.

16 A double question mark (??) signals a "marginal sentence", as proposed in Maldonado ([1999]2006: 43).
17 Observe the language economy in *detainee = detained person* and *escapee = escaped person*. Jespersen (1905: 112) observed that "*vendee* is *the person to whom a thing is sold*", an eight-word phrase expressed with one word.
18 **Este ejemplo** les podría ser más fácil de entender a los hablantes del inglés, to use an IO that is common in many languages.
19 Anna Grace Guercio (PC, December 2022) confirmed that *Laura is 20 dollars short* is what native speakers would say. She added that she thinks this phrase works only with money.
20 Speakers do not know explicitly that a verb is unaccusative (verberless), yet they know that one of the participants is an IO (requires *to* before it). David Gates, the composer of the song *It don't matter to me* (1969) failed to respect subject-verb agreement but respected the IO marking (*to*) in the title of this song.
21 *To* in English, *ad* in Latin, *kō* in Hindi languages, *a/à* in some Romance languages, *ni* in Japanese; to name a few languages belonging to different families.
22 Van Hoecke follows standard glossing. I have added single underline (verber), bold (**verbed**), and double underline (verbee) to the Latin and to the English. A false verbee (**fortibus**) is glossed as in the original but coded as a **verbed** because it passes the **verbed** entailment. An IO with *be* is marked as a verbee. The copula *be* never "assigns" accusative case (never has a DO). The other participant is always a nominative (triggers subject-verb agreement), but it will not be single-underlined. González & Whitley (1999) show that copular verbs (*ser, estar* 'be') do not have verber or **verbed**.
23 I admit that I have been teaching the IO to L2 learners of Spanish in college for more than 30 years.
24 De Andrade Berlinck (1996) does standard glossing. I have kept them, but have added the coding for verber, **verbed**, and verbee to the Portuguese sentences and to their translation into English, except for sentences with *be*, for the reason given in endnote 22.
25 De Andrade Berlinck (1996: 142) observes that many verbs with two participants whose object is an IO in Spanish is a DO in Portuguese. As González (2021, Chapter 5) shows, if the inanimate participant passes the verber entailment and the animate participant passes the **verbed** entailment, that **verbed** is often marked (replaced or pronominalized with an IO pronoun [*le/les*]) but can also be replaced or pronominalized with a DO pronoun (*la/las, lo/los*). She glosses *agradou a todos* as an IO on page 141. However, she glosses *agradou o director* as a DO on page 142. Interestingly, the verber is inanimate in both sentences (*the intelligence of the boy* and *a new decoration*). There is another twist. Portuguese *agradar* ('give pleasure') might be like *help* ('give help'). That might explain why there might be variation among native speakers. See §3.2.3.
26 This author had envisioned a chapter on two or three indirect objects, as in *no se te*[3c] *me*[3b] *le*[3a]*comas [tú] la sopa a Mafalda*[3a] 'do not eat Mafalda's soup for your own gain'. Or for her gain, because if you do so, she will not have to eat it. The word limit for this book series pushed that chapter to a future publication.
27 This article was written by 19 contributors. See references for the full list.
28 Melis (1996) did only the translation into English (third line here). I added the gloss (second line). I also coded verber, **verbed**, and verbee in French and in English.
29 He lies to him = he tells **a lie** to him. Melis (1996: 54) admits that there is an implied message. There are three participants in lying: the liar, **the lie**, and the liee. This is easier to see if we go with telling a lie: the teller, **the lie told**, and the tellee. Incidentally, there is an implied message in *talking* (you talk [**words**] to someone), in *writing* (you write [**a message**] (to) someone), in *listening* (you listen [**their words**] to someone), etc.

Against the need for more sentences with an indirect object 63

30 Rudzka-Ostyn (1996) provided glosses on the second line of each sentence. She used A for ACC, D for DAT, and N for NOM. Glossing was changed for consistency. I added the coding for verber, verbed, and verbee in Polish and in English.
31 www.actfl.org/sites/default/files/reports/Assigning_CEFR_Ratings_To_ACTFL_Assessments.pdf
32 Let me recognize here Professor Manuel García-Castellón, who proposes that instead of second (or third, or fourth, or n language), our profession should start referring to learners of OTHER language (PC, 2017).

References

Armon-Lotem, Sharon & Haman, Ewa & Jensen de López, Kristine & Smoczynska, Magdalena & Yatsushiro, Kazuko & Szczerbinski, Marcin & van Hout, Angeliek & Dabašinskienė, Ineta & Gavarró, Anna & Hobbs, Erin & Kamandulytė-Merfeldienė, Laura & Katsos, Napoleon & Kunnari, Sari & Nitsiou, Chrisa & Sundahl Olsen, Lone & Parramon, Xavier & Sauerland, Uli & Torn-Leesik, Reeli & van der Lely, Heather. 2016. A large-scale cross-linguistic investigation of the acquisition of passive. *Language Acquisition* 23(1). 27–56. https://doi.org/10.1080/10489223.2015.1047095

Belloro, Valeria. 2015. *To the right of the verb: An investigation of clitic doubling and right dislocation in three Spanish dialects.* Cambridge, UK: Cambridge Scholars Publishing. www.cambridgescholars.com/resources/pdfs/978-1-4438-8039-8-sample.pdf

Centineo, Giulia. [1986]1996. A lexical theory of auxiliary selection in Italian. *Probus* 8. 223–271. https://doi.org/10.1515/prbs.1996.8.3.223

Company Company, Concepción. 2006. El objeto indirecto. In Company Company, Concepción (ed.), *Sintaxis histórica de la lengua española. Primera parte: La frase verbal*, 479–574. Ciudad de México: Universidad Nacional Autónoma de México/Fondo de Cultura Económica. www.fondodeculturaeconomica.com/Ficha/9786071620415/F

Cuervo, María Cristina. 2003. *Datives at large.* Cambridge, MA: MIT Press. (Doctoral dissertation). www.ai.mit.edu/projects/dm/theses/cuervo03.pdf

Cuervo, María Cristina. 2010. Against ditransitivity. *Probus* 22. 151–180. DOI: 10.1515/prbs.2010.006

De Andrade Berlinck, Rosane. 1996. The Portuguese dative. In van Belle, William & van Langendonck, Willy (eds.), *The dative*, Vol. 1, 119–151. Amsterdam/Philadelphia: Benjamins. https://doi.org/10.1075/cagral.2

Dryer, Matthew S. 1986. Primary object, secondary object, and antidative. *Language* 62(4): 808–845. https://www.jstor.org/stable/415173

Gates, David. 1969. https://www.stlyrics.com/songs/d/davidgates16849/itdontmattertome2059378.html

González, Luis (H.) & Whitley, Stanley. 1999. "Lo es": Un clítico anómalo en la teoría de roles. *Hispania* 82. 298–308. https://doi.org/10.2307/346431

González, Luis H. 2021. *The fundamentally simple logic of language: Learning a second language with the tools of the native speaker.* London: Routledge. www.routledge.com/9780367688318

González, Luis H. 2022. *Understanding and teaching reflexive sentences in Spanish.* London: Routledge. https://www.routledge.com/9781032101873

Jespersen, Otto. 1905. *Growth and structure of the English language*. Leipzig: B. G. Teubner. https://archive.org/details/growthstructure0000jesp_s4f8

Maldonado Ricardo. [1999]2006. *A media voz. Problemas conceptuales del clítico se*. México, DF: Universidad Nacional Autónoma de México. www.iifilologicas.unam.mx/chiifl9/doku.php/a_media_voz

Melis, Ludo. 1996. The dative in modern French. In van Belle, William & van Langendonck, Willy (eds.), *The dative*, Vol. 1, 39–72. Amsterdam/Philadelphia: Benjamins. https://doi.org/10.1075/cagral.2

Pelletier, Francis Jeffry. 1994. The principle of semantic compositionality. *Topoi* 13. 11–24. https://doi.org/10.1007/BF00763644

RAE/ASALE (Real Academia Española y Asociación de Academias de la Lengua Española). 2010. *Nueva gramática de la lengua española. Manual*. Bogotá: Editorial Planeta Colombiana S.A. www.rae.es/obras-academicas/gramatica/manual-de-la-nueva-gramatica

RAE. 2022. https://dle.rae.es/ayudar.

Rudzka-Ostyn, Brygida. 1996. The Polish dative. In van Belle, William & van Langendonck, Willy (eds.), *The dative*, Vol. 1, 341–394. Amsterdam/Philadelphia: Benjamins. https://doi.org/10.1075/cagral.2

Van Hoecke, Willy. 1996. The Latin dative. In van Belle, William & van Langendonck, Willy (eds.), *The dative*, Vol. 1, 3–37. Amsterdam/Philadelphia: Benjamins. https://doi.org/10.1075/cagral.2

Van Valin, Robert D., Jr. & Lapolla, Randy J. 1997. *Syntax: Structure, meaning and function*. Cambridge: Cambridge University Press. ISBN: 9780521499156

Vendler, Zeno. [1957]1967. *Linguistics in philosophy*. Ithaca, NY: Cornell University Press.

Whitley, M. Stanley. 2002. *Spanish/English contrasts: A course in Spanish linguistics*. 2nd ed. Washington, DC: Georgetown University Press.

Whitley, M. Stanley & González, Luis. 2016. *Gramática para la composición*. 3rd ed. Washington, DC: Georgetown University Press. http://press.georgetown.edu/book/languages/gram%C3%A1tica-para-la-composici%C3%B3n-website

4 A pronoun does not double its indirect object; the latter drops when it is known information in postverbal position

4.1 Does a pronoun "double" its indirect object or does the indirect object drop when it is known information?

The observation of the presence of an indirect object pronoun (and less often that of a direct object) in addition to the indirect object (IO) or the direct object (DO) in a sentence can be traced back to Bello ([1847]1941: 240).

> Úsanse a veces las dos formas, simple y compuesta << me reveló el secreto a mí; >> <<Te ocultó la noticia a ti; >> <<los socorrieron a ellos; >> pleonasmo muy del genio de la lengua castellana, y a veces necesario, sea para la claridad de la sentencia, sea para dar viveza a un contraste, o para llamar la atención a una particularidad significativa.
>
> Sometimes, a simple form and a compound form are both used << me reveló el secreto a mí; >> <<Te ocultó la noticia a ti; >> <<los socorrieron a ellos; >> a pleonasm much in the spirit of Castilian, and sometimes necessary, be it for the clarity of the utterance, be it to highlight a contrast, or to call attention to a meaningful nuance. (Translation by this author.)

Observe that Bello refers to a simple and a compound form (*me* and *a mí*, etc.), and that he called the repetition a pleonasm. He also calls it a *redundancia* 'redundance' and *duplicación* 'duplication' (Bello ([1847]1941: 241). Judging by the title of his article, "The redundant object pronoun in contemporary Spanish" (Poston 1953), "redundant" was the term 100 years later. Marcos Marín (1978, chapter 4) still uses *pronombre redundante* 'redundant pronoun'. Jaeggli (1980: 25) observes that "the phenomenon which I shall call CLITIC doubling" began to receive a lot of attention after Kayne (1975).[1] If the wording "CLITIC doubling" was indeed first used by Jaeggli, the phrase has stuck to this day.[2] Roughly speaking, a CLITIC is an unstressed particle that is pronounced as part of a host word. The direct and the IO pronouns are clitics: *me, te, nos, os* have the same form for both a direct object and an IO clitic. *La/las, lo/los* are the direct object clitics for the third person (singular

DOI: 10.4324/9781003404521-4

and plural) and for the *usted/ustedes* form in Spanish. *Le, les* are the IO clitics for the third person singular and plural and for *ustedes* 'you, plural, formal'. This book will use *pronoun* but will keep *clitic* when quoting other scholars.

DATIVE CLITIC DOUBLING (IO PRONOUN DOUBLING) is the "duplication" of an IO (*a los huéspedes, al público, a Roberto*) with the corresponding IO pronoun (*me, te, nos, os, le, les*), as the three sentences in (1a-c) below show.[3]

(1) a. <u>Les</u>   cosió   **la ropa**   <u>a los huéspedes</u>.
(Gutiérrez Ordóñez 1999: 1872).[4]
them.DAT sewed-she.NOM **the clothes** to the guests.DAT
'<u>She/He</u> sewed **their clothes** *for her/his guests*'.
b. <u>Le</u>   cantó   **un aria** <u>al   público</u>.
(Gutiérrez Ordóñez 1999: 1872).
her/him.DA sang-she/he.NOM **an aria** to-the public.DAT
'<u>She/He</u> sang **an aria** *for the audience*'.
c. <u>Le</u>   curó   **el caballo**   <u>a Roberto</u>.
(Gutiérrez Ordóñez 1999: 1865)
her/him.DAT cured-she/he.NOM the horse.ACC to Roberto.DAT
<u>She/He</u> cured **Roberto's horse**. (Lit: <u>She/He</u> cured **the horse** *for Roberto*.)

According to many scholars (Company Company 2006: 489; Gutiérrez Ordóñez 1999: 1872; RAE/ASALE 2009: 2696; Strozer 1976: 137–144; among others), the duplicating pronoun is needed in these sentences because these verbs do not typically involve three participants; that is, these verbs do not have in their ARGUMENT STRUCTURE a subject, a DO, and an IO.[5] When an IO is added to a sentence whose verb does not typically involve one, the pronoun is needed. On the other hand, the duplicating pronoun is presumably optional in sentences with verbs that have three participants, like *give, promise, recommend, tell.* With verbs like *coser* 'sew', *cantar* 'sing', *curar* 'heal', etc., the IO is non argumental, and that is presumably the reason why they require the duplicating pronoun. We will propose a different explanation and will support it with plenty of data.

Since this book is primarily intended for teachers and students, here is a spoiler alert. This chapter is going to turn IO pronoun duplication upside down. It is going to argue that speakers are not "duplicating" an IO with its corresponding pronoun. Nor are speakers adding the IO, as Belloro (2007: 151, 2015: 66) and a few other scholars have suggested. The data presented on the tables in this chapter show that speakers do the opposite: instead of "getting doubled", the pronoun (*le* in 4c below) is always there with the IO (*a la mesa*, in 4b below), and the IO is the one that is dropped when it is KNOWN INFORMATION or world knowledge.[6] Thus, instead of IO pronoun doubling, this chapter will show evidence that the IO in full (*a la mesa*) is dropped, a rule that suggests that the pronoun (*le/les*) is there to begin with, and crucially, that it stays in the sentence rather than "doubling" its corresponding IO in full. When the IO is known information, it can be dropped, and it is dropped at least in 80% of the sentences, as Table 4.1 to Table 4.3 below show. This spoiler alert will help teachers and students follow the discussion with all the cards on the table, rather than assuming a rule that we will turn upside down a little later in our discussion.

The general understanding is that if there is an IO (a verbee) in a sentence, then it can (and more often than not must) be duplicated with the corresponding IO pronoun. As Belloro (2007: 146) put it, "Not only there are no contexts in which the dative clitic is categorically banned, but on the contrary there are many structures in which it is obligatory", a statement that represents better the "loose" optionality of IO pronoun doubling. Belloro's statement is also consistent with observations by several scholars that dative (IO) pronoun doubling is always mandatory. MC Cuervo (2003: 45) reports that Masullo (1992: 60) is, to the best of her knowledge, the first scholar to propose that IO pronoun doubling is mandatory, a statement with which she concurs. Although one can read isolated examples that presumably do not accept IO pronoun doubling, scholars who discuss some of those examples often argue that they are better with doubling. Suñer (1988: 395, ft 6) states that, "The only exception I am aware of concerns unqualified nouns". Her example is (*Les) Donaré todos mis bienes a museos.[7] Assuming that "datives usually refer to singular definite entities, and datives realized as indefinites or with generic reference are often unattested in corpora" (Company Company 2006: 503, translation by this author), that is a reasonable observation. On the other hand, Belloro (2015: 103–106) shows at least five examples without IO pronoun doubling of IOs with a **definite determiner** (*a estos países, a la juventud, al consternado camarero, a los jóvenes, a la gente del campo*). Suñer (1988: 395, ft 6) proceeds to question the claim in Jaeggli (1982: 59) that IO pronoun doubling is not possible with generics and offers the example, *Les dejaré todo mi dinero a los pobres.*

Observe also that the wording used to refer to the phenomenon (IO pronoun doubling, or, with more specialized terms, DATIVE CLITIC DOUBLING), suggests that a pronoun is added to "double" the IO. The almost universal understanding that sometimes the duplicating pronoun is optional (Aranovich [Roberto] 2011: 1; Gutiérrez Ordóñez 1999: 1872; Strozer 1976: 137–144; RAE/ASALE 2010: 677; among many others) also suggests that it is something that can be added. Perhaps the most invoked explanation for whether it must or may be present (or may be absent) in a sentence is the proposal that it is required if the IO is not part of the LEXICAL ENTRY for the verb. If a verb specifies an IO as part of its LEXICAL ENTRY (or ARGUMENT STRUCTURE), then the pronoun is presumably not needed. One can think about a verb's LEXICAL ENTRY as a "script" that presumably specifies for each verb whether it requires a DO and an IO. If the verb requires an IO as part of its lexical entry, then the doubling pronoun is not needed in sentences with that verb, but it might be present. That is a possible explanation for the putative optionality of IO pronoun doubling. If an IO is not part of the lexical entry for a verb, then sentences with that verb and with an IO will require a pronoun doubling the IO. In sentences (1a-c) above, *le/les* doubles the IO in each of these three examples from Gutiérrez Ordóñez (1999: 1865, 1872).

The following section shows that a rule of IO drop instead of a rule of IO pronoun doubling offers a much clearer picture of the somewhat confusing state of affairs described in the preceding two paragraphs.[8]

4.2 Indirect object pronoun doubling turned upside down

This section is going to provide evidence that an IO pronoun does not "double" its IO. Most scholars have proposed that the pronoun duplicates (doubles) the IO. A few scholars have proposed that the pronoun is an agreement marker that is added (or that the IO is added) when the IO has "a high degree of pragmatic salience" (Aranovich [Roberto] 2011: 96); "is the consequence of a non-topical argument requiring its nominal expression" (Belloro 2007: 151); or with "highly identifiable, topical nouns" (Weissenrieder 1995: 1). Observe that Belloro's statement is the opposite of the statements by other scholars. But the general understanding is that the unstressed pronoun is added, or that the IO is added. The data discussed below show that the pronoun does not double the IO nor is the IO added to double the pronoun. The rule at work is a rule of *IO drop*.

The proposal advanced here is that the IO pronoun is an agreement marker that is "generated" in the sentence with the IO. When the IO is known information, that IO can be left out, and it is left out more often than not. The evidence that follows shows that an IO in postverbal position is not added. That IO is DROPPED when it is known information or world knowledge.

In their study based on spoken data, Barrenechea & Orecchia (1970: 62) had an observation that appeared to have been lost in subsequent research on pronoun doubling. The lost observation is that the unstressed pronoun (the IO pronoun) is the basic object, an observation that we will state in slightly different terms in the rule proposed in (3) below. Marcos Marín (1978: 76) concurs with Barrenechea & Orecchia.[9] We will return to Marcos Marín's observation with the sentences in (20) below. Barrenechea & Orecchia (1970: 62) write:

> Los pronombres personales duplicados plantean no sólo el problema anterior de cuál es el reforzado, sino también el de la posición fija del pronombre átono (que afectará los cómputos en que intervenga la variable <<orden>>).
>
> En cuanto a lo primero, hemos comprobado que las encuestas analizadas no registran objetos representados sólo por pronombre tónico (sin forma átona conjunta), y en cambio hay centenares de casos a la inversa (751 átonos sin duplicación). Esto nos ha llevado a pensar que para reflejar verdaderamente el comportamiento de los hispanohablantes con respecto

a la duplicación de pronombres personales es necesario clasificar a los átonos como básicos y a los tónicos como realce que se les agrega.

Doubled personal pronouns not only pose the previous problem of which [one] is the reinforced, but also the problem of the fixed word order of the unstressed pronoun (which will affect the computation in which the variable <<order>> intervenes).

Regarding the first point, we have verified that the surveys we have analyzed do not feature objects that are represented only with a stressed pronoun (without an accompanying unstressed form), but rather that there are hundreds of the inverse situation (751 unstressed pronouns without duplication). This has led us to think that in order to truly reflect the behavior of speakers of Spanish regarding the doubling of personal pronouns it is necessary to classify the unstressed pronoun as the basic one and the stressed one as an emphasis added to the unstressed one. (Translation by this author)

Let us compare a rule of *IO pronoun doubling*, as in (2) with a rule of *IO drop*, as in (3). A putative rule of IO pronoun doubling requires several subrules, as §4.4.2 and §4.4.3 show. We are going to exemplify the rule in (2) with a subrule of INALIENABLE possession, which we chose for the sake of simplicity and representativity. Virtually all scholars agree that sentences in which inalienable possession is expressed require IO pronoun "doubling". INALIENABLE possession refers prototypically to parts of the body, but we will use an example from Jaeggli (1980: 62) referring to a table's leg because it is a natural and very interesting extension of inalienable possession.[10] Here are rules (2) and (3), followed by sentences (4a-e), with which we will begin to test these two rules:

(2) Rule of IO PRONOUN DOUBLING:

An IO pronoun (*le*) duplicates a postverbal IO (*a la mesa*) when the IO expresses inalienable possession.[11]

(3) Rule of IO DROP:

A postverbal IO is dropped when it is known information or world knowledge.

(4) a. *– ¿Qué pasó   a la mesa?
         what happened the table
      '*What happened the table?'
   b. – ¿**Qué** le   pasó   <u>a la mesa</u>?
      what.ACC it.DAT happened to the table.DAT
      '**What** happened <u>to the table</u>?'
   c. – <u>Marina</u> le   rompió **una pata**. (Also: <u>Le</u> rompieron **una pata**.)
      Marina.NOM it.DAT broke a   leg.ACC
      '<u>Marina</u> broke **one of its legs**'.

d. ?? – *Marina le rompió* **una pata** a la mesa.
'Marina broke **one of the table's legs** to the table'.
e. ?? – *Marina rompió* **una pata** a la mesa.

(An asterisk (*) before a sentence indicates that native speakers never or rarely utter that sentence. Two question marks (??) before a sentence means *un caso marginal* 'a marginal case', as Maldonado ([1999]2006: 43) proposed. Carlota Moreno de Benito (PC, 2021) marks with "??" sentences that most scholars would flag as ungrammatical. She observes that she has found in corpora more than a few sentences that would be flagged as ungrammatical).

Observe that (4a) is ungrammatical without the IO doubling pronoun (*le*). A la mesa is new information in (4b), but it is known information in (4c). If we ask speakers to rank the answers in (4c-e) from best to worst, most speakers will agree that (4c) is the best answer. The "pieces of information" *Marina*, *rompió* 'broke', and **una pata** 'a leg' are new, and they must be in the answer. Speakers can intuit that (4d) has a piece of information that we already know (*a la mesa*). As for (4e), speakers might say that it sounds somewhat weird, but that they cannot figure out what the problem is. There is known information (*a la mesa*) and we are missing the IO pronoun (*le*). If we double the IO (*a la mesa*) with a pronoun (as the rule in 2 implies), we end up with (4d). The problem is that (4d) is not the best answer for (4b). By looking at all these sentences, we can see that the rule in (2) predicts that the best answer for (4b) is (4d). It is not. On the other hand, the rule in (3) predicts that the best answer for (4b) is (4c). That is the correct prediction. In theory, speakers would "start with" (4d), but then they would drop *a la mesa* because it is known information.

In addition to the observation that (4c) is uncontroversially the best answer for (4b), and therefore that sentence (4c) is what the rule in (3) predicts, there is strong additional evidence to corroborate that (3) is the rule at work. If the rule in (2) were the rule at work, there should be many sentences similar to (4d); if the rule at work is (3), there should be many sentences similar to (4c). The data in the tables that follow this next paragraph are clear evidence that the rule at work is (3).

The omission of *a la mesa* in (4c) is similar to the omission of *ella* 'she' in (5c). Native speakers omit the subject pronoun *ella* 'she' in sentences similar to (5c) much more often than they say or write it when they are adding a comment about a participant mentioned in the previous sentence, provided there is no change in reference.

(5) a. *Ayer   conocí   a la nueva Presidenta   de la universidad.*
       yesterday met-I.NOM to the new   President-FEM of the university
       'Yesterday, I met the new President of the university'.

b. *Ella es una bióloga molecular.*
   she is a   biologist molecular
   'She is a molecular biologist'.
c.   *Es una bióloga molecular.*
   (She) is a   biologist molecular
   'She is a molecular biologist'.

Table 4.1 Frequency of indirect object pronoun alone, indirect object pronoun + indirect object, and indirect object alone (Vázquez Rozas 2006: 84)

Clitic only	9,727	78.66%
Clitic + full form	1,654	13.38%
Full form	1,085	8.77%
TOTAL	12,466	100%

Table 4.2 Indirect object pronoun alone (clitic), indirect object doubling (cl doubling), and indirect object (NP) alone (Belloro 2007: 141)

VERB	ENCODING			TOTALS
	Clitic	CL-DOUBLING	NP	
Decir 'say, tell'	52	7	0	59
Dar 'give'	43	7	1	51
Contar 'tell'	26	2	0	28
Preguntar 'ask'	15	2	0	17
Pedir 'ask for'	7	0	1	8
Enseñar 'teach'	4	0	0	4
Regalar 'give'	3	1	0	4
Pasar 'pass'	2	1	0	3
Entregar 'deliver'	1	1	0	2
Mostrar 'show'	1	1	0	2
Comprar 'buy'	0	0	1	1
Recomendar 'recommend'	0	1	0	1
TOTALS	154	23	3	180
PERCENTAGES	85.6%	12.8%	1.7%	100%

Table 4.3 Frequency of the forms of the indirect object (Weissenrieder 1995: 173)

FORM	TOTAL/%	EXAMPLE
Vag + Ø	632/75%	Le pide disculpas (p. 11)[12]
Vag + Pro	32/4%	... Le está haciendo bien a ella (p. 30)
Vag + NP	130/16%	Le grita de todo a la chica (p. 215)
Ø + NP	38/5%	Pide al ordenanza un café doble (p. 231)

Vag = Verb and Agreement Particle

The evidence is clear. With the rule in (2), there is no reason to expect sentences with the pronoun alone. That rule would predict that 79.6% of the sentences in the data in Vázquez Rozas (2006: 84) and 85.6% in the data in Belloro (2007: 141) are not sentences in Spanish. Or that the number of sentences like those should be close to 0%. Surprisingly, these data from several scholars show that in fact, between 80% and 90% of sentences in Spanish with a verbee have the pronoun corresponding to that verbee, but the verbee is not in the sentence. The rule in (3) predicts that those sentences should be sentences in Spanish. It also predicts that the verbee is known information in at least 80% of sentences in Spanish. We will retake this discussion and a review of some of the proposals on IO pronoun doubling after a short explanation of DIFFERENCIAL OBJECT MARKING, a concept that will help readers understand better the concept of DATIVE MARKING; that is, a mark that indicates to the listener/reader that a given participant is a verbee (an IO). In terms of González (2021), the presence of an IO pronoun in a sentence (*me, te, le, nos, os, les*) means that one of the participants is a verbee. Interestingly, that participant is in the sentence only approximately 10% of the time, but the IO pronoun is close to 100% of the time in the sentence, at least 80% of the time alone. Consider the following observations in Company Company (2006: 504):

> Ello confirma que la manifestación preferida y no marcada del OI en español en cualquier periodo es un pronombre átono, mayoritariamente *le*, esto es, un OI que hace referencia a una entidad singular ya presentada e identificable en el texto, humana y definida, propiedades semánticas estas que respaldan el carácter altamente topical de los DAT ya comentado.
>
> It confirms that the preferred and unmarked expression of the IO in Spanish in any period is an unstressed pronoun, mostly *le*; that is, an IO that refers to a singular entity, human and definite, already introduced and identifiable in the text, semantic properties that support the highly topical nature of the DAT(ives) already discussed. (Translation by this author)

Thus, if the unstressed pronoun is the most common expression of the IO in Spanish, as the data show and as Company Company (2006: 504) observes, speakers are neither duplicating an IO with a pronoun when that IO is "highly topical" or "salient" nor are they adding that IO. On the contrary, the evidence in this section shows that speakers *are dropping* the IO when highly topical, salient, identifiable, etc.

This section has shown that a rule of postverbal IO drop (the rule in 3) explains why at least 80% of the sentences in tables 4.1 to 4.3 has only the IO pronoun, a state of affairs difficult to explain with a rule of IO pronoun doubling (the rule in 2). The following sections will address some of the problems raised at the end of §4.1.

4.3 Is accusative *a* (personal *a*) the same as the *a* that introduces an indirect object?

Consider (6a-l). Observe the presence of personal *a* and the use of an IO pronoun (*le*) or a DO pronoun (*la*). Observe also that *Paula* is the **surprised**, not a "true" surprisee (different from the **surprised** – see §2.2), because the surprisee = **surprised**. Roberto is a true "healee" because he is different from the "healed" (**the horse**). Roberto is the benefactee of the healing of his horse. Remember that a verbee is the participant who gets something, loses it, or owns it. It is uncontroversial that Roberto's horse belongs to him. Comparable sentences with *importar* 'matter to' are provided for the reader to see that *sorprender* 'surprise' has verber (la noticia) and **verbed** (**a Paula**) and not **verbed** (**la noticia**) and verbee (a Paula), like *importar*. Translations for the sentences in (6) are provided in (7) so readers can see the sentences in Spanish without the distraction of the translation.

(6) a. La noticia sorprendió **a Paula**.   (cf. *La noticia importó a Paula.*)
 b. La noticia le sorprendió **a Paula**.   (cf. **La noticia** le importó a Paula.)
 c. *A Paula la* sorprendió la noticia.   (cf. **A Paula la importó la noticia.*)
 d. *A Paula le* sorprendió la noticia.   (cf. A Paula le importó **la noticia**.)
 e. *A Paula sorprendió la noticia.   (cf. **A Paula importó la noticia.*)
 f. *La noticia sorprendió Paula.   (cf. **La noticia importó Paula.*)
 g. **Paula** se *sorprendió*.   (cf. **Paula se importó.*)
 h. **Paula** está sorprendida.   (cf. **Paula está importada.*)
 i. Le   curó **el caballo** a Roberto. (Ex. in Gutiérrez Ordóñez 1999: 1865)
    her/him.DAT cured the horse   for Roberto
    '(Someone) Cured Roberto's horse'.
 j. #Curó el caballo   **a Roberto**.
    cured the horse.NOM to Roberto.ACC
    (Lit: '#The horse cured **Roberto**'.)
 k. La veterinaria   le   curó **el caballo** a Roberto.
    the veterinarian.NOM him.DAT cured the horse for Roberto
    'The veterinarian cured Roberto's horse'
 l. Le   curó **el caballo**   Roberto.
    him.DAT cured the horse.ACC Roberto.NOM
    'Roberto cured **his horse**'.

Translation into English of the preceding sentences:

(7) a. The news surprised **Paula**.   (cf. *The news mattered Paula.)
 b. The news surprised **Paula**.   (cf. **The news** mattered to Paula.)
 c. *To Paula her[ACC] surprised the news.   (cf. * The news mattered Paula.)

d. *To Paula her[DAT] surprised <u>the news</u>. (cf. To Paula, the news mattered to her.)
e. *To Paula surprised the news. (cf. *Paula mattered the news.)
f. *The news surprised to Paula. (cf. *The news mattered Paula.)
g. **Paula** was surprised. (cf. *Paula mattered herself.)
   (Passive voice with SE in Spanish)
h. **Paula** is surprised. (cf. *Paula is mattered.)
   [Resultative: she is in a state of "surprisingness"] [Resultative: she is in a state of "matterness")
i. <u>Le</u> curó **el caballo** <u>a Roberto</u>. (Ex. in Gutiérrez Ordóñez 1999: 1865)
   (Someone cured Roberto's horse for him)
j. #<u>The horse</u> cured **Roberto**.
k. <u>The vet</u> cured **Roberto's horse**.
   (<u>The vet</u> cured **his horse** <u>for Roberto</u>) (his horse = Roberto's horse)
l. <u>Le</u> curó **el caballo** <u>Roberto</u>. (= <u>Roberto</u> <u>le</u> curó **el caballo**. ≠ <u>Le</u> curó **el caballo** <u>a Roberto</u>.)

The personal *a* in (6a-d) tells us that Paula is the **surprised**, not the <u>surpriser</u>. Paula is not an IO, as sentences (6b,d) seem to suggest. The point of (6a-h) is to show that *sorprender* 'surprise' has <u>surpriser</u> and **surprised**. Paula is a false "surprisee" (See § 2.2). The option to use *le* instead of *la* is a rule of general *leísmo* in Spanish, a rule proposed in González (1997, 2021: 31). The rule, of course, applies to *la, las, lo, los* and expresses them as *le(s)*. This use of *le* for *la* is not the dialectal *leísmo*, mostly from central and northern Spain. It is general *leísmo*. It is a rule attested in 22 out of 22 Spanish-speaking countries, and it is a rule also attested in many other languages in the world.[13] This rule MARKS an animate **verbed** as if it were a <u>verbee</u> when the <u>verber</u> is inanimate.[14]

The choice of the example with Paula is evidence that the marker *a* that introduces IOs is the same so-called accusative *a*. That is true historically not only in Spanish; it is also true in several other languages (from different language families) with DIFFERENTIAL OBJECT MARKING, as observed in Aissen (2003: 446), Aranovich [Roberto] (2011: 99), Bossong (1991: 158, 2021: 37), RJ Cuervo ([1847] 1941: 114), Fábregas (2013: 5, 11, 32), García (1975: 336), Laca (2006: 427), among many others.[15] RJ Cuervo ([1847]1941: 114) had already observed that the mark of accusative (DO) and dative (IO) was the same in "common nouns": *azotaron al ladrón* 'they flogged the thief', *dieron cincuenta azotes al ladrón* 'they gave 50 lashes to the thief'.

The reader will notice the *a* in (6a,k). It is the same *a*. In terms of <u>verber</u>, **verbed**, and <u>verbee</u>, we can say that *a* marks (indicates) non <u>verber</u>. To simplify somewhat, the marker *a* is required (or highly preferred) when there might be some difficulty in distinguishing <u>verber</u> from **verbed**, as shown in González (2021, Chapter 3). As Alsina (1993: 454) observes, "a case distinction between subjects and nonsubjects is much less necessary than a case distinction among nonsubjects". We now turn to the need to distinguish a verbee from a **verbed**.

There is no explicit subject in (6i). It is known information. The listener/reader processing sentence (6i) knows who cured Roberto's horse. Then, the question is, why is *le* doubling a Roberto? Might it be because *curar* 'heal' is not a verb with an IO in its lexical entry? There is a better explanation. *Le* is there because the IO pronoun indicates that the participant to which it refers is an IO (i.e. it is marked with the dative case), and it is always there to begin with. When that IO is new information, the IO is also in the sentence. The IO pronoun is there to distinguish the verbee (a Roberto) from the **verbed** (**el caballo**). What would happen if *le* were not there? The sentence would be (6j), which would mean that the horse was doing the healing and Roberto is the one who got healed. That is not the intended meaning in (6i). Vets cure horses all the time because they are in the business of healing; equines do not really plan their lives with the ultimate goal of entering the health profession. Sentence (6k) has the explicit subject that was left out in (6i). It is easier for non-native speakers of Spanish to see verber, **verbed**, and verbee in this sentence. Sentence (6l) has the verber "EXTRAPOSED" (expressed at the end of the sentence). It means something very different from (6i-k). It means that Roberto is the vet (the healer) and *le* is an IO pronoun doubling a verbee identifiable by the listener/reader. That is, the verbee in (6l) is known information.

With this understanding of (6a-l), I would like to propose a two-tier verber/**verbed**/verbee theory of DIFFERENTIAL OBJECT MARKING in Spanish:

(8) Two-tier verber/**verbed**/verbee theory of differential object marking in Spanish:

   a. The marker *a* in a sentence indicates that the participant is not the verber.
   b. An IO pronoun (coindexed with the participant that does not pass the **verbed** entailment) distinguishes the verbee from the **verbed**.

After this discussion, readers who go back to the sentences in (4a-e) and (6a-l) will understand them better. They will understand better the difference between (6i) and (6l), for example; why (4d,e) are unlikely sentences in Spanish as answers to (4b); why the sentences with an asterisk are sentences that native speakers rarely or never utter; etc.

4.4 Postverbal verbee drop (when known information/ world knowledge) encompasses several rules of indirect object pronoun "doubling"

This section reviews several rules of IO pronoun doubling and shows how the rule in (3), repeated below for convenience in (10), accounts for what those rules account for. This section will also make more precise two relatively vague statements in RAE/ASALE (2010: 321). The first one is that an IO pronoun doubling an IO when the IO is in postverbal position is "very frequent". The second statement is that IO pronoun doubling is "mandatory with some predicates".

The data in Table 4.1 to Table 4.3 suggest that both the IO pronoun and the IO are "generated" by the grammar. In other words, that the underlying sentence is a sentence with both the pronoun and the IO. Then, if the IO is known information, it is dropped. Before we turn to that rule again, consider the question in (9a) and five possible answers:

(9) a. Did you wash your car yesterday?
　　b. Yes.
　　c. I did.
　　d. Yes, I did.
　　e. Yes, I washed it.
　　f. Yes, I washed my car yesterday.

Most speakers of English will agree that (9f) is the least likely answer to (9a). The most likely answers are probably (9c-d). The answer in (9e) is what is probably taught to second language learners of English in beginning and intermediate classes. Some speakers might answer with (9b). The most likely answers have something in common: known information is not repeated.

Based on the data in Table 4.1 to Table 4.3 and on sentences (1), (4), and (9), a rule of IO drop can be formulated as in (3), repeated below as (10) for convenience:

(10) Rule of verbee drop (= Rule of IO drop):
　　　A postverbal verbee is dropped when it is known information or world knowledge.

Before we proceed to review some proposals on IO pronoun doubling, let us explain why the modifier *postverbal* is needed in rule (10). When a **verbed** (a DO) or a verbee (an IO) is preverbal in Spanish, it requires a pronoun doubling it.[16] As Keniston (1937: 83) put it:

> The object pronouns are used in Spanish even when there is a noun or another pronoun expressed as the direct or IO of the verb. This practice may be due in part to the fact that Spanish word order is so flexible that the object of the verb may precede the verb; and under such circumstances the use of the object pronoun serves to indicate that the noun which begins the clause is the object rather than the subject.

Keniston is anticipating what linguists would call TOPICALIZATION; that is, the expression of a postverbal constituent in preverbal position, the position of the TOPIC of the sentence in many languages, Spanish being one of them. When the topicalized constituent is the DO or the IO, that topicalization requires a pronoun doubling the corresponding object.

Sentences (11b,d) are DO (**verbed**) topicalization. Sentence (11e) is IO (verbee) topicalization. Observe that the verbee is "doubled" with me. However, there is no need for "doubling" in (11f) because a mí is predictable from me, and a mí is not topicalized. The same explanation covers the absence of a mí in (11d). Sentence (11c) is a sentence that most native speakers do not utter. Sentence (11h) is an INTRANSITIVIZATION WITH SE, as proposed in González (2022, Chapter 2). Observe that a single rule that a preverbal participant that is not the verber requires a pronoun to indicate that it is not the verber covers **verbed** topicalization (11b,d), verbee topicalization (11e), and intransitivization with SE (11h).

(11) a. *Compré   esta camisa   ayer.*
bought-I.NOM this shirt.ACC yesterday
'I bought **this shirt** yesterday'.
b. *Esta camisa la   compré   ayer.*
this shirt.ACC it.ACC bought-I.NOM yesterday
(Lit: '**This shirt**, I bought it yesterday'.)
c. ??Esta camisa compré ayer.[17]
d. *Esta camisa me   la   regaló mi esposa.*
this shirt-ACC me.DAT it.ACC gave my wife
Lit: '**This shirt**, me my wife gave it to me'.
e. *A mí   me   regaló mi esposa   esta camisa.*
to me.DAT me.DAT gave my wife.NOM this shirt.ACC
f. *Mi esposa me regaló esta camisa.*
'My wife gave me this shirt'.
g. ??*Mi esposa me regaló esta camisa a mí.*
'??My wife gave me this shirt to me'.
h. *Esta camisa se   compró ayer.*
this shirt.NOM se.REFL bought yesterday
'**This shirt** was bought yesterday'.
i. *Esta camisa compró ayer.
Lit: *'This shirt bought yesterday'

As we review below some of the main proposals to account for IO pronoun doubling, the reader will observe that the rule in (10) covers all those rules. In the introduction, it was observed when IO pronoun doubling was mandatory: (1) when the IO is expressed preverbally, (2) when it is not part of the lexical entry of the verb (i.e. the IO is "non argumental"), (3) with verbs like *gustar* (comparable to *matter to* in English), and (4) presumably when the IO is a stressed pronoun. The following discussion shows that an IO pronoun co-occurs mandatorily with its IO only when the IO is *preverbal*. That is a rule of ATYPICAL (NON-DEFAULT) WORD ORDER in Spanish, as observed in Keniston (1937: 83). We will show that an IO pronoun duplicates an IO in *postverbal* position only when the latter is new information. This is, of course, another way of stating the rule in (10). There is an advantage to the rule of (10), however. The rule in (10) implies that the IO pronoun and the IO in full are in the UNDERLYING sentence, and that the latter can be dropped. When the IO drops, the IO pronoun remains. That is the case in 80% to 90% of sentences in Spanish. A rule of IO pronoun doubling does not have an explanation for the presence of an IO pronoun alone in a sentence.

4.4.1 Three rules of indirect object doubling with a pronoun in Gutiérrez Ordóñez (1999)

Gutiérrez Ordóñez (1999: 1871–1872) formulates three rules for IO duplication with a pronoun. According to him, IO pronoun doubling is mandatory:

First, when the prepositional constituent (the IO) precedes the clitic (the topicalized argument – *a su hijo* in 12b).[18] The prepositional constituents are the phrases *a Lucas* and *a su hijo* in his examples below. The prepositional constituent is a phrase introduced by *a* that is presumably an IO. As Chapter 2 showed for similar sentences, the topicalized object in (12a) is a DO because it passes the **verbed** entailment.

(12) a. *A Lucas*   no le   *interesan <u>nuestros asuntos</u>*.[19]
to Lucas.ACC no him.DAT interest   our   business
'**Lucas**, <u>our business</u> do not interest **him**'.
b. <u>*A su hijo*</u>   *le*   *escribe por fax*.
to his son.DAT him.DAT writes by fax
'<u>He</u> writes <u>to his son</u> by fax'. (Lit: <u>His son</u>, he writes <u>to him</u> by fax.)

The object **a Lucas** in (12a) is not an IO. It is a **verbed** (cf. <u>Nuestros asuntos</u> no interesan **a Lucas**; **Lucas** se interesa; **Lucas** está interesado). Sentence (12a) is general *leísmo*. **A Lucas** is really the **verbed** (el interesado 'the interested' – not really the "interestee", because the "interestee" = interested). It is duplicated because it is a TOPICALIZED **VERBED**. *Le* is preferred over *la* due to the animacy alignment (See González 2021, Chapter 3). As sentences (13a-d) show, speakers of Spanish will agree that the pronoun will still be *le/les*, even if the **verbed** is feminine and plural, a state of affairs not predicted by dialectal *leísmo* in central and northern Spain. Speakers for whom *las* in (13a) or even (13b) might be hard to accept, should not have any trouble accepting (13c,d). The equivalent sentences in (14a-d) with *importar* 'matter' will no doubt persuade some of those with some skepticism regarding (13a,b). Granted, the frequency of (13a) with *las* and the frequency of sentence (13b) is close to Ø, but not Ø, as examples (68a) and (70a,b) from

Gutiérrez Ordóñez (1999: 1879–1880) show. Observe also an example from *El País* (a newspaper from Spain) in endnote 19.

(13) a. *A estas damas*   *no les*   */las*   *interesan*
to these ladies.ACC not them.DAT /them.ACC interest
<u>*nuestros asuntos*</u>.
our matters
'These ladies are not interested in our matters'.
(Lit: **These ladies,** <u>our matters</u> do not interest them[dat]/**them**[acc].)
b. <u>*Nuestros asuntos*</u> *no interesan* **a estas damas**.
Our matters   no interest   to these ladies
'Our matters are of no interest <u>to these ladies</u>'.
(These ladies do not have an interest in our matters.)
c. **Estas damas** *no <u>se</u> interesan en nuestros asuntos*.
'These ladies are not interested in our matters'.
d. **Estas damas** *no están interesadas en nuestros asuntos*.
'These ladies are not interested in our matters'. (Resultative sentence)

(14) a. <u>*A estas damas*</u> *no les/(*las) importan* **nuestros asuntos**.
'**Our matters** do not matter <u>to these ladies</u>'. (cf. *Our matters do not matter these ladies.)
b. *<u>Nuestros asuntos</u> no importan **a estas damas**.
*'Our matters do not matter these ladies'.
c. ***Estas damas** no se importan en/con nuestros asuntos. (Passive voice/ event reading)
'These ladies are not mattered in/with/by these matters'.
d. ***Estas damas** no están importadas en nuestros asuntos.
*'These ladies are not mattered by these matters'. (Resultative sentence)

The rule at work in (12a,b) is a rule of TOPICALIZATION that signals MARKED (ATYPICAL) WORD ORDER to highlight a piece of information. If the grammar already has a rule of **verbed** or <u>verbee</u> topicalization (as explained with the sentences in 11), there is no need for this first rule in Gutiérrez Ordóñez (1999: 1871) when the prepositional constituent (*a Lucas*, *<u>a su hijo</u>*) precedes the pronoun (*le*/<u>*le*</u>) and the verb, as in (12a,b).

Second, when a prepositional constituent contains a STRESSED pronoun (Gutiérrez Ordóñez 1999: 1872). *Ella* and *nosotros* are the stressed pronouns in (15a,b) below. *Le* and *nos* are the unstressed ones.

(15) a. <u>*Le*</u>   *gusta <u>a ella</u>*   *mucho más*. (1999: 1872).
her.DAT like   to her.DAT much   more
'She likes it much more'. (cf. **Gusta a ella mucho más*.)
b. <u>*Nos*</u>   *envió*   *<u>a nosotros</u>* **los negativos**. (In photography)
us.DAT sent-she/he.NOM to us.DAT the negatives.ACC
'<u>She</u>/<u>He</u> sent <u>us</u> **the negatives**'. (cf. **Envió a nosotros los negativos*.)

The observation that a pronoun doubles an IO "in full" (*a ella, a nosotros*) is reasonable if one assumes that the full IO requires at times a doubling pronoun. There is another explanation. The "doubling pronoun" is an agreement marker that goes hand-in-hand with the IO "in full". In sentences (15a,b), there is an IO pronoun (*le, nos*) "doubling" the IO (*a ella, a nosotros*) because the IO is new information; therefore, the doubling pronoun and the IO appear in the sentence. Consider this exchange:

(16) a. – *¿Por qué llamaste* **al abuelo?**
 why called-you.NOM to-the grandpa.ACC
 'Why did you call **Grandpa**?'
 b. – *Porque le llegaron los resultados de los exámenes de sangre.*
 because him.DAT arrived the results of the tests of blood.
 NOM
 'Because **the results of his blood tests** arrived'. (Lit: **The results** . . . arrived for him.)
 c. ?? – *Porque le llegaron los resultados de los exámenes de sangre al abuelo.*
 (An unlikely answer due to the repetition of al abuelo [known information in postverbal position] in the answer.)
 d. ?? – *Porque le llegaron los resultados de los exámenes de sangre a él.*
 (Same as 16b, but al abuelo is replaced with *a* + stressed pronoun.)
 e. ??*Porque llegaron los resultados de los exámenes al abuelo.*
 f. *Porque llegaron los resultados de los exámenes del abuelo.*
 because arrived.NOM the results of the tests of-the grandpa
 'Because the results of Grandpa's tests arrived'.

Llegar 'arrive' is not a tri-actantial verb like *dar* 'give'. It is VERBERLESS (UNACCUSATIVE in terms of subject and DO). Interestingly, **things** *arrive for people*. That is, the recipient of something that arrives in the mail is the benefactee (or malefactee) in Spanish, in English, and presumably in many other languages. Sentences (16c,d) are rarely uttered by native speakers because the verbee (al abuelo/ a él) is known information. Its repetition is totally unnecessary. Observe that the IO would be a stressed pronoun (*a él*). Hardly any native speaker of Spanish will have *a él* in (16b). It is not in the sentence because it is known information. But we have the "duplicating" pronoun. Thus, an *a + pronoun* is in the sentence not because it is a stressed pronoun but when it is new information. Since the rule in (10) is already part of the grammar, a rule that *a + pronoun* must be doubled is not needed. Furthermore, with that rule it is impossible to explain why the "duplicating" pronoun can appear in a sentence by itself (as in 16b). Since *llegar* 'arrive' is not a verb with an IO in its ARGUMENT STRUCTURE, it would require "doubling". That explains why native speakers very rarely utter sentences like

(16e). Sentence (16f) is possible if *el abuelo* is expressed as a possessive phrase (*del abuelo* 'Grandpa's') and not as a verbee (*al abuelo* 'for Grandpa'). Notice, however, that (16f) is not a smart answer to (16a), neither in Spanish nor in English.

An IO is left out when it is known information whether that IO is a full IO (*a los huéspedes* or *al público*, as in 1a,b repeated below as 17a,) or a pronoun (the *a él* that nobody hears or sees in 16b). The reader can go back now to sentences (11d,f) and confirm that if we needed an IO in full, it will be *a mí* 'to me'. That IO can be in the sentence, particularly, if we have to highlight the givee (e.g. ***esta camisa me la regaló mi esposa a mí***, *no te la regaló a ti* 'my wife gave **this shirt** to me; she did not give **it** to you'). But the IO is more often than not omitted: the IO in full is *a mí* 'to me', unequivocally.

Third, when the IO is non argumental (Gutiérrez Ordóñez 1999: 1872):

(17) a. <u>Les</u>   cosió   **la ropa**   *a los huéspedes*.
        (Gutiérrez Ordóñez 1999: 1872)
        them.DAT sewed-she/he.NOM **the clothes** to the guests.DAT
        '<u>She/He</u> sewed **their clothes** for her/his guests'.
    b. <u>Le</u>   cantó   **un aria** *al público*. (Gutiérrez
        Ordóñez 1999: 1872).
        her/him.DAT sang-she/he.NOM **an aria** to-the public.DAT
        '<u>She/He</u> sang **an aria** for the audience'.

In *el resto de los casos* 'the rest of the cases', a duplicating pronoun is optional.

If readers are asked to compare which rule would offer a better explanation for (17a,b), a rule stating that IO pronoun doubling is mandatory with a non-argumental IO or a rule that we already have in the grammar stating that an IO pronoun and an IO both co-occur in a sentence if the IO is new information, but that the IO is left out when it is known information, the answer is clear. A rule of non-argumental IO requires a distinction between argumental and non-argumental IOs. See § 4.5 for some evidence against the need for such a distinction. More importantly, a rule of known-information drop accounts for the co-occurrence of the pronoun and the object or the presence of the pronoun alone in argumental and in non-argumental IOs without the need to know this distinction.[20] The rule in (10) explains why there are so many sentences with an IO pronoun, but without the IO, an observation that is very difficult to account for with a putative rule of IO pronoun doubling. Furthermore, a rule of known-information drop is already part of the grammar of most languages (perhaps of all languages) in the world. It is very easy to explain to a second language learner that a los huéspedes and a Marina are NEW information in (18a) but KNOWN information in (18b). It is also remarkable that in (18b),

Marina is a silent (dropped) verber and a los huéspedes a silent (dropped) verbee. Consider this exchange:

(18) a. – ¿Por qué le   están pagando **dinero**   los huéspedes
         why   her.DAT are paying money.ACC the guests.NOM
    a Marina?
    to Marina.DAT
    'Why are the guests paying **money** to Marina?
  b. – Porque les   cosió   **la ropa**.
       because them.DAT sewed-she.NOM the clothing.ACC
       (cf. Porque ~~Marina~~ les cosió **la ropa** ~~a los huéspedes~~.)
       ('Because she sewed **their clothes** for them'.)
  c. ?? – Porque les cosió **la ropa** a los huéspedes.
  d. # – Porque cosió la ropa **a los huéspedes**.

It is uncontroversial that the best answer to (18a) is (18b). Sentence (18c) repeats known information. Sentence (18d) is missing the IO pronoun, and its absence invites the interpretation that *la ropa* is the sewer (the one doing the sewing) and *a los huéspedes* is the sewn. People are stitched up all the time by physicians and nurses, but clothes never sew people. In (17a), the *les*, which agrees with a los huéspedes, tells the listener/reader that a los huéspedes is the benefactee of the sewing. **La ropa** passes the **verbed** entailment. It is very interesting that *los huéspedes* is the payer in (18a), but the sewee in (18b), yet listeners can keep track of them. More importantly, speakers duly notice the change in roles. I would like to claim that they do so because they know the meaning of *pay*, *sew*, *the guests*, and *Marina*, and the possible combinations of these words in meaningful sentences in the language. Notice that *Marina* is encoded as the "silent" subject of *cosió* 'sewed', *les* keeps track of a los huéspedes as the benefactee in (18b), which need not be mentioned, even if its function changes from payer in (18a) to sewee in (18b). Crucially, the only piece of information that is not represented in a "veiled" way (by a PRONOUN!) in (18b) is *la ropa* 'their clothes', the NEW information. If she (*Marina*) undergoes subject pronoun drop in 18b (pro-drop is the specialized term in linguistics), *les* allows the speaker to do verbee drop, when that verbee is known information. Thus, in this answer, only one out of three different pieces of information (participants) is explicitly represented (**the verbed**). The two other pieces (verber and verbee) are represented via agreement markers (*Marina* is "read off" from the verb ending in *cosió* 'sewed' and *a los huéspedes* is "read off" from *les*).

To summarize this section, a rule that a verbee in postverbal position is dropped from a sentence when it is known information accounts for the last two rules proposed by Gutiérrez Ordóñez (1999: 1871–1872) that we have just discussed. When the verbee (or the **verbed**) is preverbal, the object does not drop. A rule of postverbal verbee drop accounts for the fact that a verbee pronoun appears in a sentence by itself at least 80% of the time, a state of affairs that "mandatory" or "very frequent" IO pronoun "duplication" predicts should not be the case. The third rule (discussed as the first rule) is needed as a rule of MARKED (i.e. ATYPICAL) WORD ORDER in the grammar of Spanish and presumably of many other languages.

4.4.2 Rules of <u>indirect object</u> (and direct object) pronoun doubling in RAE/ASALE (2010)

According to RAE/ASALE (2010: 319–321), IO (and DO) object pronoun doubling is mandatory, per the three rules discussed below.

First, when these complements (objects) are represented by stressed personal pronouns preceded by the preposition *a*:[21]

(19) a. ***La***   *vieron*   ***a ella***. (cf. *Vieron a ella)
her.ACC saw-them.NOM to her.ACC
'They saw **her**'.
b. ***Nos***   *quieren*   ***a ti***   *y*   ***a mí***. (cf. **Quieren a ti y a mí*)
us.ACC love-they.NOM to you.ACC and to me.ACC
'They love both of us, you and me'.
c. ***Las***   *leí*   ***todas*** *de un tirón*.
them-FEM.ACC read-I.NOM all   of one fell swoop
'I read them all in one fell swoop'.
(More frequent than *Leí todas de un tirón* [RAE/ASALE 2010: 320].)
d. <u>*Me*</u>   *permitieron **eso***   <u>*a mí*</u>. (RAE/ASALE 2010: 319). (cf.
**Permitieron eso a mí*)
me.DAT permitted that.ACC to me.DAT
'They permitted **that** <u>to me</u>'.

It is true that an IO (and a DO!) that is expressed with *a* + stressed pronoun (*a ella, a ti, a mí*, and even *todas* in 19c) is always doubled, if the group *a* + *stressed pronoun* shows up in the sentence. However, if that *a* + stressed pronoun is known information or can be "recovered" by world knowledge, the "doubling" pronoun is in the sentence, but the phrase *a* + *stressed pronoun* should not be, as the following examples show. (Translations by this author).

(20) a. *– **Me** extraña* <u>*que no llame*</u>*.* (Ex. in RAE/ASALE 2010: 2656 [§35.1c])
'It baffles me that she does not call'. (I find it strange that she does not call.)
(No need for *a mí*. It is world knowledge in context.)
b. *– No* <u>*te*</u> <u>*me*</u> *acerques*. (Ex. in RAE/ASALE 2010: 2657 [§35.1e])
'Do not come close to me'.
c. *– <u>Se</u> <u>nos</u> alejan **las oportunidades***. (Ex. in RAE/ASALE 2010: 2657 [§35.1e])

'Opportunities escape us'.
d. *– No se me ponga nerviosa.* (Ex. in RAE/ASALE 2010: 2657 [§35.1e])
'Do not get nervous on me'.
e. *– No **me** pongo nerviosa.*
'I do not get nervous'.
f. *– Fusíleme a **mí** también.* (Goytortúa, 1949; quoted en Marcos Marín 1978: 76)
g. *– Fusíleme también.* (Marcos Marín 1978: 76)
shot-me also
'Shot me also'.
h. * *– Fusile a mí.* (Marcos Marín 1978: 76)
shot to me
'Shot me'.
i. *– No te permito juzgarme sin oír una explicación.*
'I am not going to allow you to judge me without hearing my explanation'.
(*A ti* and *a mí* are predictable from *te* and from *me*. No need to express neither of them.)
(Observe how forced the sentence with "doubling" sounds: ??No te permito a ti **juzgarme a mí sin oír una explicación**.)
j. *– ¿Me permites que te diga **algo**?* (cf. ??*¿Me permites a mí **que te diga algo a ti**?*)
'Will you let me **tell you something**?'
(*tell you something* is **the let (allowed)**. You is the "letter" (allower). I is the teller; you, the tellee; and **something** is **the told**).

The *a + stressed pronoun* should not show up in the sentence if it is known information or world knowledge, as the sentences in (20), (except for 20h), suggest. Therefore, a stressed personal pronoun does not necessarily require doubling, as many scholars have claimed that it does (Aranovich [Roberto] 2011: 28, 96; Belloro 2007: 146; Fábregas 2013: 48; Gutiérrez Ordóñez 1999: 1872; RAE/ASALE 2010: 319; Suñer 1988: 394, 401; among many others). Aissen (2003: 446), Gómez Torrego (1999: 304), and Marcos Marín (1978: 76–79) are three of very few scholars who have observed that stressed pronouns do not always require doubling. Marcos Marín (1978: 76) concurs with Lenz (1925: 83–84) that the true complement is the clitic alone, since the clitic suffices, as the examples in (20a-j) show.[22] It might be that *a + stressed pronoun* is new information rather frequently, and that might be the reason why it seems to scholars that it is always doubled with the corresponding IO pronoun. In that sense, it should be in the sentence.

Observe that if we work with the hypothesis that one of the two elements is added (the unstressed pronoun or the IO/stressed pronoun), we must answer the question of which one is the basic and which one is the "doubled" (the duplicator and the duplicated). On the other hand, under an analysis in which one of them is deleted when known information, that is a question that does not even have to be asked.

Observe that the *a mí* or *a ti* in (20i,j) is similar to the subject that is omitted in most commands, both formal and informal. Strikethrough indicates that the pronoun is almost always omitted.

(21) a. *¡Muévete (tú) a la derecha!*
'(You-informal) Move to the right!'
b. *¡Muévase (usted) a la derecha!*
'(You-formal) Move to the right!'
c. *¡Muévanse (ustedes) a la derecha!*
'(You-plural/formal) Move to the right!'
d. *¡Moveros (vosotras/vosotros) a la derecha!*
'(You-plural/informal) Move to the right!
e. *¡Movámonos (nosotras/nosotros) a la derecha!'*
'Let us move to the right!'

Attentive readers might ask why *todas* 'all of them' (feminine) is not omitted in (22c). There is some truth to the observation that an object that is a pronoun might need to be present because it makes processing easier. There is some redundancy in language, and this is a good example. Observe, however, the following question and the possible answers, including (22g), an answer that almost no native speaker will utter:

(22) a. *¿Leíste **todas las noticias** que te mandé sobre la Unión Europea?*
'Did you read **all of the news** that I sent you about the European Union?'
b. **Las**   leí   **todas** de un tirón.
them.ACC read-I.NOM all   in one fell swoop
'I read all of them in one fell swoop'.
c. **Las leí todas.**
d. **Todas.**
e. *De un tirón.*
f. **Todas las leí.**
g. *Leí todas.²³

I do not like to speculate. But I cannot resist to share a conjecture that came to me as I was pondering the sentences in (22) to account for the *las* doubling *todas*. Might it be that a second possible explanation for (22c) is a deletion of a topicalization, as in (23b)? I leave that possibility open for further research.

(23) a. *¿Leíste **todas las noticias** que te mandé sobre la UE?*
b. *Las noticias las lei todas.*
'The news, I read **them all** (= all of them).

c. **Las leí todas.**
'I read **them all**'. ('I read **all of them**'.)

The way to explain what we have known until now about IO (or DO) pronoun doubling is looking at the sentences in a more "holistic" way. Readers will realize that IO pronoun doubling seems to be what is going on when one looks at sentences one at a time, as when one looks at sentences like those in (17a,b) in isolation. A different picture emerges when one looks at sentences in a more holistic way, as in (18), where we have discourse context and in (20a-g, i,j), where we have world knowledge to help us in processing sentences without unnecessary repetitions.

According to RAE/ASALE (2010: 320), there is an exception with verbs of direction, like *acercarse* 'approach':

(24) Se   acercó   a mí. (Ex. 47 in RAE/ASALE 2010: 320).[24]
    se.REFL approached to me
    'She/he approached me'.

There is a possible explanation for the apparent exception to pronoun doubling in (24). *A mí* can have two interpretations here. The first one is that it is an IO; the second one, it is a locative, as pointed out in RAE/ASALE (2009: 2678): "No son excepciones ejemplos como *se acercó a mí* (§35.6b,c), ya que en estos casos el grupo preposicional es un complemento locativo que alterna con un dativo átono". ('Examples like *she/he approached me* are not exceptions, since in these cases the prepositional group is a locative object that alternates with an unstressed dative'. Translation by the author.). *Se acercó a mí* [locative] is similar to *se acercó donde mí* 'he approached to the place where I was standing'.

Second, with DISLOCATED CONSTRUCTIONS (= **verbed** and verbee topicalization). These are TOPIC INITIAL CONSTRUCTIONS; that is, the prepositional group provides thematic information that is expressed before the verb (RAE/ASALE 2010: 321). Sentence 25a (35a in RAE) is **VERBED** TOPICALIZATION; 25b (35b in RAE) is VERBEE TOPICALIZATION.

(25) a. ***El periódico   lo   compra mi hijo.***
       the newspaper.ACC it.ACC buys   my son.NOM
       '**The newspaper**, my son buys **it**'.
    b. *A Laura   le   robaron   el bolso.*
       to Laura.DAT her.DAT stole-them.NOM the purse.ACC
       'Laura was stolen **her purse**'.

An attentive reader might ask what happens with a **verbed** that is topicalized, but the verbee is not. IO pronoun "doubling" is "mandatory". Remarkably, that follows if the pronoun is always in the sentence (regardless of whether the IO is or not), as the rule in (10) predicts. Observe also that an L2 learner who knows that a verbee which is new information must be expressed in the sentence will be able to predict that *se* (a form of *le*) must also be in the sentence if the IO pronoun is part of the sentence to begin with (because it is new information).[25] That prediction is correct. It is also the case that this rule must be explicitly stated if we use the rules by RAE, but it is not needed with the rule in (10). (The rule would be that there is IO pronoun doubling even when the **verbed** is topicalized).

(26) ***El periódico***   *se*   **lo**   vendió   *a mi hijo*   *la señora*
     The newspaper se.DAT lo.ACC sold-she to my son.DAT the lady
     del quiosco.
     at-the kiosk.NOM
     '**The newspaper**, the lady at the kiosk sold **it** to my son'.
     'The newspaper was sold to my son by the lady at the kiosk'.
     (cf. *El periódico lo vendió a mi hijo la señora del quiosco.)

In fact, the obligatoriness of the dative pronoun here (*le* → *se*) is evidence that the IO pronoun is in the underlying representation of the sentence. That is, it is an agreement marker that is "generated" when the IO is generated; therefore, there is no rule of IO pronoun doubling, but a rule of IO drop.

We have already shown that a rule of **verbed** or verbee topicalization is already part of a theory of word order in the grammar of Spanish.

Third, when the IO goes after the verb, IO pronoun doubling is *very frequent* with IOs. It is mandatory with *some predicates* (RAE/ASALE 2010: 321):

(27) a. *No le*   dijeron   **la verdad**   *a su*   *madre*.
      no le.DAT told-they the truth.ACC to their mother.DAT
      'They did not tell the truth to their mother'.
   b. *No le*   dieron   **importancia** *al*   *asunto*.
      no le.DAT gave-them.NOM importance to-the matter
      'They did not pay any attention to the matter'.
   c. *Le*   duele **el pie**   *a Felipe*. (cf. *Duele el pie a Felipe).
      le.DAT hurt the foot.NOM to Felipe.DAT
      'Felipe's foot is hurting'.

As in Gutiérrez Ordóñez (1999: 1885), doubling is optional elsewhere, although "en los casos de alternancia opcional, la elección puede tener consecuencias semánticas" (RAE/ASALE 2010: 677). ["In those cases in which there is optionality, the choice can have semantic consequences". Translation by this author]. Readers will observe that sentences (27a,b) are sentences with an argumental IO. Those sentences should not show IO pronoun doubling. They do because the IO is new information. No need for speakers to know whether any verb includes an IO as part of its argument structure.

As RAE/ASALE (2010: 672), put it, non-argumental IOs can be omitted without affecting, in general, the grammaticality of the sequence. They can also be added, in practice, *a cualquier verbo con dos argumentos* 'to any verb with two arguments' (Company Company 2006: 537). Furthermore, the argumental character of a participant does not imply that it is mandatory (RAE/ASALE 2010: 672). Therefore, if argumental IOs are not mandatory, and non-argumental ones can be freely added or omitted, there does not seem to be much substance to the notion of IO argumenthood. However, if that IO is new information, it will be in the sentence, regardless of whether it is argumental or not.[26]

This third rule by RAE is helpful neither to L2 learners nor to native speakers. A rule that states that IO pronoun doubling with postverbal IOs is "very frequent" begs the question as to what "very frequent" means. Likewise for the statement that IO pronoun doubling is mandatory with "some predicates". The rule in (10) allows us to explain precisely what "very frequent" really means and what those "some predicates" are.

Table 4.1 to Table 4.3 answer the question of frequency. IO pronoun doubling is not very frequent at all. It is 13.38% in Vázquez Rozas (2006: 84). Part of that 13.13% might be verbee topicalization. That 13.13% might also include some *leísmo* (dialectal and general). If we consider verbee topicalization as a rule of word order that is already part of the grammar (a reasonable proposal), postverbal IO pronoun doubling might be closer to 7% than to 13.13%. The 12.88% in Belloro (2007: 141) is consistent with the data in Vázquez Rozas, but it also probably includes verbee topicalization and some *leísmo* general. It is also reasonable to conjecture that doubling of the IO in postverbal position in Belloro's study might be closer to 7% than to 12.88%. Remember that IO pronoun doubling occurs not only when the verbee is topicalized; it also occurs when the **verbed** is topicalized, if there is a verbee in the sentence, as in (26) above. That is another factor that might push that 7% even a little lower, if the verbee is known information.

Let us turn to the observation by RAE/ASALE (2010: 321) that IO pronoun doubling is "mandatory with some predicates". González (2021, Chapter 5) explains exactly what the "some predicates" that require clitic doubling are. There is a caveat, though. Those predicates have the IO pronoun and the IO in full ONLY when the IO is new information. Of course, if the IO is topicalized, both the IO and the IO pronoun must be present. Let us turn to the example *Le duele **el pie** a Felipe* 'Felipe's foot is hurting' from RAE/ASALE (2010: 321) into a question and let us provide several possible answers:

(28) a. ¿***Qué*** le pasó a Felipe?
      What.NOM le.DAT happened to Felipe
  b. Le duele **un pie**.
      him.DAT hurts a foot.NOM

'His foot is hurting'. (One of his feet is hurting.)
c. ??Le duele un pie a Felipe. (Marginal, as an answer to 28a.)
d. *Duele un pie a Felipe.

Sentence (28b) is evidence that the IO pronoun is always there and that the IO in full is left out when it is known information. Sentence (28d) is evidence that the IO pronoun distinguishes the verbee from the verbed and that the IO in full can be omitted but le/les cannot. After this discussion, the theory of differential object marking in (8) above should make more sense for every reader. Of course, if *a Felipe* is topicalized, both the verbee and the pronoun appear in the sentence: *a Felipe le duele un pie*. (cf. **A Felipe duele un pie*.).

The "*some predicates*" to which RAE/ASALE (2010: 321) refers are the true members of the *gustar* class in Spanish, as discussed in González (2021, Chapter 5). Those are verberless verbs, one of whose two participants – typically the animate – is a verbee and the other participant is a **verbed**. Interestingly, the benefactee/malefactee of those 40 verbs do not accept doubling with a DIRECT OBJECT PRONOUN (*la/las*; *lo/los*), clear evidence that those objects are true verbees (true IOs):

(29) a. *A Felipe le duele un pie/le apetece un café/le gustan las frutas/le llegó una carta*.
'Felipe's foot is hurting/Felipe feels like having a cup of coffee/Felipe likes fruits/a letter arrived for Felipe'.
(*LE* indicates that *a Felipe* is a verbee.)
b. **A Felipe lo duele un pie/*lo apetece un café/*lo gustan las frutas/*lo llegó una carta.
(*LO* would indicate that *a Felipe* is a **verbed**.)

Remember that Gutiérrez Ordóñez (1999: 1872–1874) has a rule that IO pronoun doubling is required with non-argumental IOs (IOs that are used with verbs that do not ordinarily require an IO, like *sew, break, eat*, etc.), but that the presence of the pronoun is not mandatory with argumental IOs (the IO of verbs that are ordinarily used with an IO, like *give, tell, promise, recommend*, etc.). It is revealing that the two examples given in RAE/ASALE (2010: 321) are argumental and they have clitic doubling (*no le dijeron la verdad a su madre; no le dieron importancia al asunto* [our sentences in 27a,b]).[27] Indeed, one of those examples is the prototypical verb with an argumental IO, *give*, the verb from which the dative case originated (Butt 2006: 14). The other is *decir* 'tell', the prototypical verb of communication. The participant marked with dative case indicates the animate who receives the gift or gets the information. Although some examples seem to allow the omission of an IO pronoun with postverbal IOs of verbs that require an IO, those sentences are few, and that situation might be acceptable only with isolated sentences. Consider the questions in (30a,e) and the answers to each of them:

(30) a. *¿**Qué** le   dio   el abuelo   a la abuela*
       what her.DAT gave the grandpa.NOM to the grandma.DAT
       en Navidad?
       for Christmas
       '**What** did Grandpa give Grandma for Christmas?'
  b. **Dio una bufanda.*
  c. *Le   dio   **una bufanda**.*
     her.DAT gave.he.NOM a   scarf.ACC
     'He gave her **a scarf**'.
  d. ??*Le dio una bufanda a la abuela.*
     ??'He gave a scarf to Grandma'. (Marginal as an answer to 30a.)
  e. *¿A quién   le   dio   el abuelo   **una bufanda***
     to whom.DAT her.DAT gave the grandpa.NOM a   scarf.ACC
     en Navidad?
     for Christmas
     To whom did Grandpa give **a scarf** for Christmas?
  f. *Se   la   dio   a la abuela.*
     se.DAT it.ACC gave-he.NOM to the grandma
     'He gave **it** to Grandma'.
  g. **La dio a la abuela.*
  h. #*Dio a la abuela.*
     #'He gave Grandma'.

Observe that (30b) is not ungrammatical per se. But it is a non sequitur as an answer to (30a). There is missing information. We are missing one out of three participants. The *le* in (30c) helps the listener/reader keep track of the verbee; but if the verbee is known information, all the listener/reader needs is the pronoun (*le*). Sentence (30d) is a sentence that speakers of the language do not produce because there is an unnecessary repetition. Notice that (30f) has the IO pronoun (*se*) and the IO. But since the IO is new information, it must be there. Sentence (30f) is an ENTAILMENT of the rule in (10); that is, if a postverbal IO is to be dropped when known information, it is entailed that it is left in situ when it is new information. Sentence (30h) would mean that *a la abuela* is the **given** (the gift), not the givee. No Grandma would appreciate that. Sentence (30g) would be sentence (30h) in River Plate Spanish, if Rioplatense speakers would say or do that. I think no Rioplatense speaker would say or do that.

To summarize this section, the rules discussed under first and third by RAE/ASALE (2010: 319–321) can be accounted for with the rule in (10). The rule of IO (or DO) pronoun "doubling" when the object is preverbal is a rule of marked (atypical) word order that is already part of the grammar of Spanish.

4.4.3   Other rules of indirect object pronoun "doubling"

Belloro (2007: 146–147) reviews six rules for IO pronoun doubling. She covers the three rules just covered by Gutiérrez Ordóñez (1999) and RAE/ASALE (2010): Clitic doubling is mandatory if the IO occurs preverbally, if the IO is a stressed pronoun, and if it is non argumental. We have seen that the only rule on the right track is the rule of an IO that is preverbal. That is a rule of word order. We have shown that there is "doubling" (i.e. non dropping of the IO!) with a stressed pronoun and with IOs (be they argumental or non argumental) if the IO is new information in postverbal position.

Belloro (2007: 146–147) also discusses other rules proposed by other scholars. There is presumably IO pronoun doubling if the IO is a semantic experiencer (as in 31a below); if it is realized by a proper name (Company Company 2006: 491, 536), as in (31b); or if it involves inalienable possession, as in (31c) below (Fernández Soriano 1993). The rule of IO pronoun doubling with inalienable possession can be traced back to Jaeggli (1980: 62), as shown in §4.2, and in endnote 10.

(31) a. *A Paula*   *Ø/le   alegró   <u>la noticia</u>. (Ex. 141c in Belloro 2007: 147)[28]
to Paula.DAT   /le.DAT made happy the news.DAT
'The news pleased Paula'.
b. *Ø/<u>Le</u>   contó   <u>a Gisela</u> **su secreto**   **más**
le.DAT told-she.NOM Gisela   her secret.ACC most
íntimo. (Ex. 141e in Belloro 2007: 147)
intimate.DAT
'She let Gisela in on her most intimate secret'.
c. *Ø/<u>Les</u>   dolía   **la cabeza** <u>a todos los que vieron</u>
les.DAT hurt.3S the head   all the ones   saw-they.NOM
<u>esa película</u>. (Ex. 141f in Belloro 2007: 147)
that movie.DAT
'All the people who saw that movie had a headache'.

Sentence (31a) can be explained with the rule of preverbal (in)direct object. Many readers will now realize that **A Paula** is not a true <u>verbee</u>; she is a **verbed** (<u>la noticia</u> alegró *a Paula* , *A Paula la* alegró <u>la noticia</u>, **Paula** <u>se</u> alegró, **Paula** está alegre, and even **Paula** fue alegrada por la noticia). A putative role of experiencer is not needed with <u>verber</u>, **verbed**, and <u>verbee</u>. Sentence (31b) can be explained if the proper name is new information. If the proper name is known information, it is not unnecessarily repeated. We already discussed a case of inalienable possession and showed that the IO is needed if it is new information, omitted if known information, and crucially, that the pronoun is always there. Demonte (1995: 20) claims that the order V DO IO does not require pronoun doubling (*Di el libro a María*). However, with the order

V IO DO (%*Di a María el libro*), the doubling pronoun is required. Speakers polled by Demonte reported that the structure (V IO DO) "asks for the clitic" (Demonte 1995: 20). An explanation that the IO is present when it is known information accounts for the presence of the proper name if it is new information, whether it is before or after the DO. And without the need to stipulate whether that new information is a proper name.

Sentence (31c) can be explained because *doler* 'hurt' is a *gustar* verb; that is, a verb with **verbed** and verbee, and the verbee is postverbal and apparently new information.

Section 4.4 (4.4.1 to 4.4.3) has shown that the rule in (10) encompasses the rules by Gutiérrez Ordóñez (1999), by RAE/ASALE (2010), and several rules proposed by other scholars. More importantly, the rule in (10) shows that an IO pronoun does not really duplicate an IO. On the contrary, both are part of the sentence, and the latter drops when it is known information.

4.5 Some evidence against the distinction between argumental and non argumental indirect objects[29]

Although RAE/ASALE (2009: 2659) accepts the distinction, it also points out that some scholars have questioned it. As RAE/ASALE (2010: 672), put it, non-argumental IOs can be omitted without affecting, in general, the grammaticality of the sequence. They can also be rather freely added (Company Company 2006: 537). Furthermore, the argumental character of a participant does not imply that it is mandatory (RAE/ASALE 2010: 672). RAE is quoted just for convenience, but some of these are observations that go back centuries. The Spanish grammarian Correas (1626) had already pointed out that the same verb can be used transitively or intransitively. *El niño comió* **uvas** 'the child ate **grapes**' and *el niño comió* 'the child ate' were his examples, perhaps a tribute to *El lazarillo de Tormes*.[30] Now we can add that countless verbs can be used ditransitively as well, as when an IO can be added, even to a verb like *be*: *Después de este libro*, *a muchos estudiantes les será mucho más fácil entender el IO* 'after this book, **understanding the IO** will be much easier for many students'. By "reverse engineering", **di**transitive verbs can be used not only transitively but also **in**transitively, as when one can say that *el abuelo no ha dado del cuerpo hoy* 'Grandpa has not had **a bowel movement** today', a sentence that is still transitive in English but intransitive in Spanish. The verb *deliver* (a verb with deliverer, **delivered**, and deliveree) can easily be used intransitively: *gourmet restaurants do not deliver*.

Interestingly, if a participant that is introduced with a preposition in Spanish (a verbee that requires *a* in Spanish, even when it accepts "IO shift") can be rather freely added or deleted, and the meaning of that prepositional phrase is the sum of the meaning of the preposition plus the meaning of the NP (a verbee), that prepositional phrase behaves very similar to any other prepositional phrase in the language, as shown in González (2021: 59–61), drawing on a proposal in Davis (2001: 119). Therefore, the distinction between argumental and non-argumental IOs is hard to maintain. More importantly, such a distinction does not have much to contribute to our understanding of a verbee in a sentence.

As Belloro (2007: 146) put it, "Not only there are no contexts in which the dative clitic is categorically banned, but on the contrary there are many structures in which it is obligatory". If the pronoun is a marker of an IO, it should be there; and the IO can be omitted when known information. This will be consistent with the presence of the pronoun alone in more than 80% of the sentences in Table 4.1 to Table 4.3, discussed in this chapter. The IO alone is at the most in 12% of sentences with an IO. Indeed, as the evidence shows, the pronoun is a marker of an IO that is "generated" in the sentence, and it is not "added". Nor is the IO added to a sentence with an IO pronoun when there is a need for clarity.

Let us use sentence (18), repeated below as (32) to review that the rule at work is a rule of deletion of known information.

(32) a. – ¿*Por qué le están pagando* **dinero** *los huéspedes*
      Why   her.DAT are paying money the guests
    a Marina?
    to Marina.DAT
    'Why are the guests paying **money** to Marina?'
  b. – *Porque les cosió* **la ropa**. (cf. Porque ~~Marina~~ les cosió **la ropa** a los huéspedes.)
    Because them.DAT sewed the clothing.ACC
    'Because she sewed **their clothes** for them'.
  c. –??Porque les cosió **la ropa** a los huéspedes.
    '??Because for them she sewed their clothes for the guests'.
  d. –*Porque cosió la ropa **a los huéspedes**.
    *'Because their clothes sewed **the guests**'.

Can a learner of Spanish as an L2 determine payer, **paid**, and payee in (32a)? Absolutely, if they know the meaning of each word in those sentences. Particularly because most L2 learners who would come across sentences like these will be at least at the Intermediate Low to Intermediate High level in the ACTFL scale (A1.2 to B1.2 in the CEFR scale).[31] Or L2 learners who have been exposed to exercises like those in Chapter 2 and Chapter 4 in this book. Can learners understand the shift in role from (32a) to (32b)? The payee in (32a) is the (implicit) sewer in (32b). The payer in (32a) is the (implicit) sewee in (32b). What is omitted? The known information, even if the role changes from the question to the answer. What is present in the answer? The new information. Observe also that *pagar* 'pay' is a verb with three participants. The omission of *le* (and **dinero** 'money') in (32a), might invite an interpretation in which *Marina* is the one given as payment. Readers are invited to go back to (18a-d) to review some observations about those sentences which need not be repeated here.

To summarize, the rule in (10) requires native speakers and L2 learners to know what known information is, a task that language users do all the time, intuitively and implicitly. Current rules of IO pronoun doubling appear to require the distinction between argumental and non-argumental IOs, a distinction challenged by several scholars, and a task that seems monumental vis-à-vis the task of knowing what known information is.[32]

There are other arguments against the distinction between argumental and non-argumental IOs. However, the few points outlined above should suffice. In fact, a further exploration of the issue will be an excellent project for a final paper in a class. That paper might result in an MA thesis, and perhaps in a PhD dissertation.

4.6 Verbee drop in the classroom

The realization that the phenomenon at play is the dropping of the IO and not the doubling of it with an IO pronoun (as many scholars have proposed) or the adding of the IO (as some scholars claim) goes back only to 2020. Therefore, this author is just beginning to test the main point of this chapter in the classroom. The other main proposals in this book have been tested for ten to thirty years now. As for some indirect evidence that this will work in the classroom, I can share a comment by a linguist (Jerid Francom) during a presentation of this proposal at a talk in 2021: "The connection between IO drop(ping) and subject drop is very interesting". Both the verber and the verbee are overwhelmingly animate, definite, and perhaps even singular to a great extent.

Moreover, as mentioned in § 4.3, whether an IO is known information or new information is an easy task for most L2 learners of Spanish (or any other language) to grasp. A few simple question-and-answer examples, like the exchanges in (4, 9, 16, 18, 28, etc.) suffice to help learners understand whether the IO is new or known information, and why the IO is omitted, if the latter.

After students are introduced to verber, **verbed**, and verbee, they realize that tracking them is a lot easier than tracking subject, DO, and IO, as sentences (10a-d) in Chapter 2, repeated here as (33a-d) show:

(33) a. We bought **new pajamas** for our children.
 b. We bought our children **new pajamas**.
 c. **New pajamas** were bought for our children (by us).
 d. Our children were bought **new pajamas** (by us).

Furthermore, once students can distinguish a **verbed** from a true verbee, as explained in Chapter 2, their understanding of objects in a sentence is as good, and for some better, than the current understanding of objects by many native speakers, teachers, and scholars. A college professor of Spanish (who is also a

A pronoun does not double its indirect object 95

native speaker and a PhD) said during a talk about these issues by undergraduate students of Spanish in college in October 2016, "These students have an understanding of DO and IO that is better than that of many native speakers". That teacher is Dr. Carmen Pérez Muñoz.

I believe that the simplicity and intuitiveness of this proposal will help many teachers and language learners from many different languages understand better who does **what** to whom in a sentence; that is, to track verber, **verbed**, and verbee, the heart of language understanding and production.

4.7 Conclusions

Does an IO pronoun "doubles" its IO? If that were the case, there would not be an explanation for the 80% to 90% cases of IO pronoun without an IO in a sentence. Does the IO gets dropped when known information? If that is the case, we have an explanation for the 80% to 90% cases of IO pronoun without an IO in a sentence. How do we account for the presence of the IO pronoun? It is always there, as the marker of an IO to differentiate the verbee from the **verbed**, and perhaps from the verber. After all, a verbee shares with the verber the properties of being high in animacy (human) and definiteness, two properties that distinguish both from the **verbed**, which tends to be inanimate and indefinite.

Listening to the numbers was crucial in arriving at the proposal in this chapter. Although this chapter is perhaps the longest chapter this author has ever written, I made an effort to keep it short. And simple. Table 4.1 to Table 4.3 were enough to make the main point. There are literally dozens, perhaps hundreds of tables in research on the IO. I resisted the temptation to include many of them. A few of those tables should be revised to distinguish a postverbal (or preverbal) object doubled with *le/les*, but which is a **verbed**, not a verbee. That is one of the issues for further research. With a caveat. Determining whether an object is a **verbed** or a verbee is relatively easy most of the time. It might be a challenge, even for scholars, a few times. Consider these two sentences:

(34) a. *Esta propuesta les sorprenderá **a muchos investigadores***.
    'This proposal will surprise many researchers'.
    'Many researchers will find this proposal surprising'.
   b. *Esta propuesta les ayudará a muchos aprendices*.
    'This proposal will help many researchers'.
    'Many researchers will find this proposal helpful'.
    'Many researchers will find this proposal helpful to them'.

At first sight, these two sentences are similar. They are not.

(35) a. *Esta propuesta sorprenderá **a muchos investigadores***.
   b. ***A muchos investigadores** les sorprenderá esta propuesta*.

    c. **A muchos investigadores los** sorprenderá <u>esta propuesta</u>.
    d. **Muchos investigadores** <u>se</u> sorprenderán *(con esta propuesta)*.
    e. **Muchos investigadores** *fueron sorprendidos por esta propuesta*.
    f. **Muchos investigadores** *están sorprendidos*.
    g. <u>Esta propuesta</u> *es* <u>la sorprendedora</u>. (cf. #Esta propuesta es la sorprendida.)
    h. **Los investigadores** son **los sorprendidos**. (cf. #Los investigadores son los sorprendedores).
    i. <u>Esta propuesta</u> *los sorprenderá* **a muchos investigadores**. (River Plate Spanish?)

It is uncontroversial that *sorprender* has <u>surpriser</u> and **surprised**. The verb *ayudar* 'help' is more challenging. Perhaps because it has the verb *give* inside it: *help <u>someone</u>* = *give **help** <u>to someone</u>*.

(36) a. ??<u>Esta propuesta</u> ayudará a muchos aprendices.
    b. <u>A muchos aprendices</u> <u>les</u> *ayudará* <u>esta propuesta</u>.
    c. ??A muchos aprendices los ayudará esta propuesta.
    d. ??Muchos aprendices se ayudarán (con esta propuesta).
    e. ??Muchos aprendices fueron ayudados por esta propuesta.
    f. ??Muchos aprendices están ayudados.
    g. <u>Esta propuesta</u> *es* <u>la ayudadora</u>. (cf. #Esta propuesta es la ayudada.)
    h. **Los aprendices** *son* **los ayudados**. (cf. #Los aprendices son los ayudadores).
    i. ??Esta propuesta los ayudará a muchos aprendices. (River Plate Spanish?)
    j. <u>A muchos aprendices</u> <u>se</u> <u>les</u> *ayudará con esta propuesta*.

An important difference is that *ayudar* is *dar<u>le</u>* **ayuda** <u>a alguien</u>. The same way that *agradecer* is *dar<u>le</u> gracias <u>a alguien</u>*, *perdonar* is *perdonar<u>le</u> [una ofensa] <u>a alguien</u>*, *servir* is *servir<u>le</u> [la comida] <u>a alguien</u>*, *obedecer* es *obedecer<u>le</u> [las órdenes] <u>a alguien</u>*, etc. See González (2021, Chapter 5, for a more detailed discussion). That difference explains why the sentences in (36) are not clearly comparable to those in (35). Neither are they comparable to those in (37). If a reader is thinking that (36) and (37) are kind of frustrating, that reader might have a point. However, that reader should also ponder how much harder this would be without the coding (<u>verber</u>, **verbed**, <u>verbee</u>). Above all, how much harder this would be with DO and IO. Here is (36) with *dar* **ayuda** :

(37) a. <u>Esta propuesta</u> <u>les</u> *dará* **ayuda** <u>a muchos aprendices</u>.
    b. <u>A muchos aprendices</u> <u>les</u> *dará* **ayuda** <u>esta propuesta</u>.
    c. *A muchos aprendices los dará ayuda esta propuesta.
    d. *Muchos aprendices se darán ayuda (con esta propuesta).
    e. *Muchos aprendices fueron dados ayuda con esta propuesta.

A pronoun does not double its indirect object   97

f. *A muchos aprendices se les dará **ayuda** con esta propuesta.*
g. ??Muchos aprendices están dados ayuda.
g. *Esta propuesta es la dadora de ayuda.* (cf. #Esta propuesta es la ayudada.)
h. *??Los aprendices son los dados ayuda.* (cf. #Los aprendices son los ayudadores).
(cf. *A los aprendices fue a quienes se les dio **ayuda**.*)
i. *Esta propuesta los dará ayuda a muchos aprendices.

It seems counterintuitive to conclude with a few sentences for which an explanation is not offered, other than with grammaticality judgements that cry for some data from corpora. The good news is that in most sentences, distinguishing a false verbee from a true verbee is clearly easy with verber and **verbed**, as Chapter 2 showed (§2.2). There are very, very few cases that will be as challenging as the one in (36–37). It also seems that the conclusions are not the place to write two to five pages about these last two sentences and some of their variations. However, it seems appropriate to finish this book with an invitation to others to take it from here. This book might be the first book on the IO addressed to teachers and advanced L2 learners. I hope it is not the first one for a long time. A comparable book can be written for many other languages to discuss these issues and similar ones as helpful for teachers and L2 learners as some of those discussed in this book.

4.8   Exercises (answers provided)

Exercise 1

Write sentences in the present tense with the following words. The strings within each sentence are in alphabetical order. This exercise practices the most common *gustar* verbs and most of these sentences come from writing by college students learning Spanish as an L2. Teachers can write similar exercises with verbs found in the materials for their class.

Examples

1. Doler / la cabeza / Marcos
   Answer: A Marcos le duele **la cabeza**.
2. Gustar / los impuestos / muchos ciudadanos / no
   Answer: A muchos ciudadanos no les gustan **los impuestos**.

Observe that the word order is verbee, **verbed**. The other order is possible, but the verbee, **verbed** order is the most frequent one. Even L2 learners int their second or third semester of Spanish in college recognize that native speakers would say *me gusta el chocolate* 'I like chocolate' much more frequently than *el chocolate me gusta*.

Exercises

1. Dormir en una silla / gustar / Juan / no
2. Dibujos animados / gustar / los niños y a muchos adultos
3. Estos payasos / estos sombreros / pertenecer
4. Dinero / Rosa / sobrar
5. Dinero / este empresario / faltar
6. Actriz / el guion / parecer bien
7. Algo extraño / este payaso / ocurrir
8. Doce clases / faltar / Lidia y a Sofía
9. Carlos / costar 50 euros / esa hermosa camisa
10. Nosotros / quedar un mes de clase
11. Encantar / las frutas / nosotros
12. ¿Apetecer / una taza de café / tú?
13. ¿Estos ejercicios / gustar / ustedes?
14. La tierra / no pertenecer / nosotros /; nosotros / pertenecer / la tierra (these phrases are already ordered. Your task is to write the sentence).
15. ¿Cómo / estos ejercicios / parecer / tú?

Answers to exercise 1

The answers are mostly in the present tense. Teachers can easily adapt these exercises to the most recent tense presented in the course. Some sentences highly favor ("call for") a particular tense. In fact, many of these sentences might be used to practice preterite and imperfect. In spite of the fact that these verbs are relatively abstract (they are states, which are not as prototypical verbs as activities are), it is easy to see a difference in meaning when preterite is used instead of imperfect.

1. Dormir en una silla / gustar / Juan / no > A Juan no le gusta **dormir en una silla**. (Also: **Dormir en una silla** no le gusta a Juan.)
2. Dibujos animados / gustar / los niños y a muchos adultos > A los niños y a muchos adultos les gustan **los dibujos animados**. (**Los dibujos animados** les gustan a los niños y a muchos adultos.)
3. Estos payasos / estos sombreros / pertenecer > **Estos sombreros** les pertenecen a estos payasos. (A estos payasos les pertenecen **estos sombreros**.)
4. Dinero / Rosa / sobrar > A Rosa le sobra **dinero**. (*Dinero le sobra a Rosa. A common DETERMINERLESS NOUN cannot be the subject in

preverbal position. See Suñer 1982: 209.). A DETERMINER is a definite article (el dinero), a possessive adjective (mi dinero), a demonstrative adjective (este dinero), or a quantifier (mucho/poco dinero). Quantified **verbeds** tend to follow their verbee.

5. Dinero / este empresario / faltar > A este empresario le falta **dinero**. (Also: A este empresario le hace falta **dinero**. Cf. *Dinero le falta a este empresario.)
6. Actriz / el guion / parecer bien > A la actriz le parece bien **el guion**. (**El guion** le parece bien a la actriz.)
7. Algo extraño / este payaso / ocurrir > A este payaso le ocurre **algo extraño**. (This sentence is probably better in preterite: A este payaso le ocurrió **algo extraño**. **Algo extraño** le ocurrió a este payaso.)
8. Doce clases / faltar / Lidia y a Sofía > A Lidia y a Sofía les faltan **doce clases**. (??Doce clases les faltan a Lidia y a Sofía.)
9. Carlos / costar 50 euros / esa hermosa camisa > A Carlos le costó 50 euros **esa hermosa camisa**. (**Esa hermosa camisa** le costó 50 euros a Carlos.). This sentence does not make much sense in the present tense.
10. Nosotros / quedar un mes de clase > Nos queda **un mes de clase**. (cf. A~~nosotros~~ nos queda **un mes de clase**. *A nosotros* is completely predictable from *nos*. ??Un mes de clase nos queda.)
11. Encantar / las frutas / nosotros > Nos encantan **las frutas**. **Las frutas** nos encantan. (*A nosotros* is predictable from *nos*.)
12. ¿Apetecer / una taza de café / tú? > ¿Te apetece **una taza de café**? (*A ti* is completely predictable from *te*.). (??Una taza de café te apetece.)
13. ¿Estos ejercicios / gustar / ustedes? > ¿Les gustan **estos ejercicios**? (cf. ¿~~A ustedes~~ les gustan **estos ejercicios**? = ¿Les gustan **estos ejercicios** a ~~ustedes~~? Although *les* could also refer to *ellas* or *ellos*, it is almost always clear in context whether *les* refers to *a ellas*, *a ellos*, or *a ustedes*.). (??Estos ejercicios les gustan?)
14. La tierra /no pertenecer / nosotros /; nosotros / pertenecer / la tierra > **La tierra** no nos pertenece a nosotros; **nosotros** le pertenecemos a la tierra. This is a case where *a nosotros* is needed. A case more of contrast than new information.)
15. ¿Cómo / estos ejercicios / parecer/ tú? > ¿Cómo te parecen **estos ejercicios**? (This is also a case in which the preterite might be best choice: ¿Cómo te parecieron **estos ejercicios**?).

Exercise 2

After exercise 1, you should be able to discover and correct mistakes made by learners of Spanish as a second language (L2). This exercise practices verbs like *gustar*. They have **verbee** and **verbed**. They come from writing by college students who are studying Spanish as an L2. The task of the learner is

100 A pronoun does not double its indirect object

to say or write the sentence that the student wanted to express. Answers after the exercise.

1. A muchos habitantes se gusta el país.
2. Los habitantes no les gustan la guerra.
3. Ellos no le gustan Rosa. (Intended: Rosa does not like them).
4. Ella le gusta español.
5. Tuvimos como 20 años en los cuales nadie le gusta el gobierno.
6. Todas mis amigas gustan a mi papá.
7. A otros países no les gusta a EE.UU.
8. Nadie me le gustaba.
9. Conocí otras comidas que los niños les gustan mucho.
10. Una de las mujeres piensa que las otras mujeres le gusten su esposo. (Do you see the problem? ¿Who likes whom? Does he like them? Do they like him?)
11. Si uno le gusta cocinar. . .
12. Las personas que les falta dinero. . .
13. Decidimos faltar algunos días de trabajo o de clase.
14. Miré a mi mamá. ¡Ella faltó una ceja!
15. La mayor parte de la película falta diálogo porque el protagonista es sordomudo.
16. Santiago falta lluvia entre mayo y agosto.
17. Los latinos no faltan la pasión en ninguna manera.
18. Pienso que el autor falta entendimiento sobre el humor.
19. Casi parece que el autor falta presentar el problema.
20. Yo falté dos semanas de escuela.
21. La introducción falta de una oración fuerte que capte la atención del lector.
22. La segunda y tercera parte falta la originalidad de la primera.
23. Si esta película le falta algo, es que deja de ofrecer una solución fácil.
24. Eso falta toda razón.
25. "Renovable" es lo que faltan los combustibles de hoy.
26. El artículo falta datos concretos.
27. Todos ilusionábamos mucho del concierto.
28. Los recíprocos no importan a los autores muchos.
29. Se preguntaba si las chicas solamente le gustaban a causa de su vestuario de diseño.
30. El club sobró dinero después de pagar todos los gastos del concierto.

Answers to exercise 2

1. A muchos habitantes se gusta el país. > <u>A muchos habitantes</u> <u>les</u> gusta **el país**.
2. Los habitantes no les gustan la guerra. > <u>A los habitantes</u> no <u>les</u> gusta **la guerra**. (Better: <u>A muchos ciudadanos</u> no <u>les</u> gusta **la guerra**.)

3. Ellos no le gustan Rosa. (Rosa doesn't like them.) > **Ellos** no le gustan a Rosa. (Also: A Rosa no le gustan **ellos**).
4. Ella le gusta español. > A ella le gusta **el español**.
5. Tuvimos como 20 años en los cuales nadie le gusta el gobierno. > Tuvimos como 20 años en los cuales a nadie le gustaba **el gobierno**.
6. Todas mis amigas gustan a mi papá. > A todas mis amigas les gusta **mi papá** (All of my friends like my father).
7. A otros países no les gusta a EE.UU. > A otros países no les gusta **EE.UU.**
8. Nadie me le gustaba. > **Nadie** me gustaba (I did not like anyone). A different sentence: **Yo** no le gustaba a nadie = nobody liked me.
9. Probé otras comidas que los niños les gustan mucho. > Probé **otras comidas** que a los niños les gustan mucho = Probé **otras comidas** que les gustan mucho a los niños.
10. Una de las mujeres piensa que las otras mujeres le gusten su esposo. (Do you see the problem? ¿Quién le gusta a quién? Does he like them? Do they like him? > Una de las mujeres piensa que a las otras mujeres les gusta **su esposo**. A different sentence: Una de las mujeres piensa que a su esposo le gustan **las otras mujeres**.
11. Si uno le gusta cocinar . . . > Si a uno le gusta **cocinar**.
12. Las personas que les falta dinero . . . > Las personas a quienes les falta **dinero**. Mejor: A quienes les falta **dinero**. (*A quienes* refers necessarily to people.)
13. Decidimos faltar algunos días de trabajo o de clase. > Decidimos faltar a algunos días de trabajo o de clase. (*A algunos días de trabajo* is an expression of time. That is the reason why there is no IO pronoun. *Faltar* requires *a* after it because it is a verb of movement. It is the opposite of *ir a clase*. Very interesting, is it not?)
14. Miré a mi mamá. ¡Ella faltó una ceja! > Miré **a mi mamá**. ¡Le faltaba **una ceja**! (It is clear that it is ~~A ella~~ le faltaba **una ceja**.)
15. La mayor parte de la película falta diálogo porque el protagonista es sordomudo. > A la mayor parte de la película le falta **diálogo** porque el protagonista es sordomudo.
16. Santiago falta lluvia entre mayo y agosto. > A Santiago le (hace) falta **lluvia** entre mayo y agosto.
17. Los latinos no faltan la pasión en ninguna manera. > A los latinos no les falta **la pasión** de ninguna manera.
18. Pienso que el autor falta entendimiento sobre el humor. > Pienso que al autor le falta **entendimiento sobre el humor**.
19. Casi parece que el autor falta presentar el problema. > Casi parece que al autor le falta **presentar el problema**.
20. Yo falté dos semanas de escuela. > Falté a dos semanas de clase. (*a dos semanas de clase* is an expression of time. That is the reason why there is no IO pronoun. See 13 above.)

21. La introducción falta de una oración fuerte que capte la atención del lector. > A la introducción le falta **una oración fuerte que capte la atención del lector**.
22. La segunda y tercera parte falta la originalidad de la primera. > A la segunda y tercera partes les falta **la originalidad de la primera**.
23. Si esta película le falta algo, es que deja de ofrecer una solución fácil. > Si a esta película le falta **algo**, es que deja de ofrecer una solución fácil.
24. Eso falta toda razón. > A eso le falta **toda la razón**. Tal vez mejor: Eso no tiene ninguna razón.
25. "Renovable" es lo que faltan los combustibles de hoy. > Renovable es **lo que** les falta a los combustibles de hoy.
26. El artículo falta datos concretos. > Al artículo le faltan **datos**. (Data and examples are concrete). Examples can be useful, appropriate, revealing, etc. But they are, by definition, concrete.
27. Todos ilusionábamos mucho del concierto. > A todos nos ilusionaba mucho **el concierto**.
28. Los recíprocos no importan a los autores muchos. > **Los recíprocos** no les importan mucho a los autores.
29. Se preguntaba si las chicas solamente les gustaban a causa de su vestuario de diseño. > Se preguntaba si (**él**) les gustaba a las chicas solamente a causa de su vestuario de diseño. (El chico es quien lleva ropa de diseño.)
30. El club sobró dinero después de pagar todos los gastos del concierto. > Al club le sobró **dinero** después de pagar todos los gastos del concierto.

Exercise 3

These sentences are "Englishy" ("grammar" calques from English). Most of them will be expressed with a verbee in Spanish. Write them again using a verbee. Sometimes it is necessary to change the verb. For example, if someone expresses that they *tienen miedo*, the verb *tener* is appropriate. However, if the speaker wants to express that *he tuvo miedo*, the meaning of preterite and *tener* here express the end of the fear, not the beginning. In this case, *le dio miedo* ('began to feel fear') is the meaning intended by the speaker.

1. Cuando estaba allá arriba y miré para abajo, tuve mucho miedo.
2. Primero, pidieron el dinero de Jason.
3. Andy se gana el favor de los guardias porque hace los impuestos para ellos.
4. Andy tapa el agujero con carteles de mujeres que recibió de Red.
5. Cuidaba de los niños de los amigos de mis padres.
6. Yo rompí mi dedo.
7. Una persona podía darme un golpe a mi dedo.
8. Un día encuentra el amor y este cambia toda su vida.
9. Su madre manda que Tula olvide a Lan.

10. Este diseño añade interés para el lector.
11. Puse las cadenas en las llantas del carro.
12. Enterró un cuchillo en el corazón de la persona.
13. Ya es hora de hacer unos cambios en el sistema.
14. Cuando di una mirada en el indicador de la gasolina.
15. Mi cabeza dolía mucho.

Answers to exercise 3

1. Cuando estaba allá arriba y miré para abajo, tuve mucho miedo. > Cuando estaba allá arriba, miré para abajo y me dio **mucho miedo**.
2. Primero, pidieron el dinero de Jason. > Primero, le pidieron (**el**) **dinero** a Jason. (*Le pidieron* **DINERO** *a Jason* means that they asked him for some money; *le pidieron* **EL dinero** *a Jason* means that they asked for a known and precise amount of money. The first sentence expresses *money* as part; the second, as whole.)
3. Andy se gana el favor de los guardias porque hace los impuestos para ellos. > Andy se gana el favor de los guardias porque les hace **los impuestos**.
4. Andy tapa el agujero con carteles de mujeres que recibió de Red. > Andy tapa **el agujero** con carteles de mujeres que Red le dio.
5. Cuidaba de los niños de los amigos de mis padres. > Les cuidaba **los niños** a los amigos de mis padres.
6. Yo rompí mi dedo. > Me rompí **un dedo**. Better: me fracturé **un dedo**. Me quebré **un dedo**.
7. Una persona podía darme un golpe a mi dedo. > Una jugadora podía darme **un golpe** en el dedo. (The speaker had already told the listener about a broken finger.)
8. Un día encuentra el amor y este cambia toda su vida. > Un día encuentra **el am**or y este le cambia **la vida**.
9. Su madre manda que Tula olvide a Lan. > La madre le manda a Tula **que olvide a Lan**.
10. Este diseño añade interés para el lector. > Este diseño le añade **interés** a la obra.
11. Puse las cadenas en las llantas del carro. > Le puse (**las**) **cadenas** a las llantas del carro. (If *las cadenas* have not been mentioned, the speaker uses *cadenas*. If *las cadenas* have been mentioned, the speaker uses *LAS cadenas*.)
12. Enterró un cuchillo en el corazón de la persona. > Le enterró **un cuchillo** a la persona en el corazón. (Observe how this order flows better than *le enterró* **un cuchillo** *en el corazón a la persona*. The verbee [*a la persona*] is a more central participant than the heart. *En el corazón* is a locative modifier, a more peripheral modifier than a verbee.)
13. Ya es hora de hacer unos cambios en el sistema. > Ya es hora de hacerle **algunos cambios** al sistema.

14. Cuando di una mirada en el indicador de la gasolina... Hint: think outside the box. > Cuando miré el indicador de la gasolina. Also: Cuando le eché **una mirada** al indicador de la gasolina...
15. Mi cabeza dolía mucho. > Me dolía **la cabeza** mucho. Also: me dolía mucho **la cabeza**. Also: **la cabeza** me dolía mucho.
16. Note: Four out of 15 IOs are inanimate in the preceding exercise (10, 11, 13, 14). That frequency is provocative. If it is representative, it suggests that close to 25% of IOs are inanimate in Spanish. That is an issue for further research, if it has not been done.

Notes

1 Key terms will be capitalized when their mention is particularly relevant. If they are not explained in the same paragraph, they will be explained in an endnote.
2 *Duplicación del clítico* 'duplication of the clitic' seems to be the wording in Spanish. It returned 1,350 results in Google (October 2022). *Doblaje del clítico* 'doubling of the clitic' returned 0 results. *Clitic doubling* returned 48,000 results whereas *clitic duplication* returned 740 results. Each string searched within quotes ("clitic doubling").
3 The difference between a DO pronoun (*la, las, lo, los*) and an IO pronoun (*le, les*) is "visible" only in the third person. In the other persons, the pronoun is the same, regardless of whether the object is direct or indirect (*me, te, nos, os*), or even reflexive, for that matter.
4 The verber will be underlined, the **verbed** in bold, and the verbee double underlined.
5 One can think about the ARGUMENT STRUCTURE or the LEXICAL ENTRY of a verb as a "script" that presumably specifies for each verb whether it requires a DO and an IO. Levin and Rappaport's title for their 2006 book on argument structure can be helpful in grasping the concept: *Argument Realization*. The arguments in a sentence are the core participants (subject, DO, IO). They are often mandatory, but crucially, not always.
6 The following quote from Belloro (2007: 105) shows an excellent example of world knowledge (the use of *the boss, the colleagues,* etc.) as "known information"; that is, inferences that we draw once the speaker mentions her new job:

> Thus, if a speaker mentions *a job*, then she may go on to refer to *the boss, the colleagues,* or *the salary,* marking them as definite. In this case it is the association between these entities and jobs that has rendered them "familiar" in this particular context, thus justifying the use of the definite article even for discourse entities that are, strictly speaking, new to the discourse.

7 This notation means that the sentence is ungrammatical with *les*. This author would write or say the sentence with *les*.
8 The choice between IO *drop* vs. IO *dropping* is interesting. The latter wording (dropping) seems more intuitive, as pointed out by Jerid Francom (PC, March 2021). *IO drop* parallels subject pronoun drop (pro drop), a rule that drops a subject pronoun (*they* 'ellas') when it is known information, as the strikethrough indicates below:

> En el 2022 conocí a Carolina López Chacarra y a Mimi Rhodes. ¡~~Ellas~~ Son unas golfistas del otro mundo! ('I met C López C and M Rhodes in 2022. They are out-of-this-world golf players!')

9 This observation goes back at least to Lenz (1925: 83–84), as Barrenechea & Orecchia (1970: 61–62) pointed out.
10 These are examples in Jaeggli (1980: 62):
   i.   *Le duele la cabeza a Juan.* (*Duele la cabeza a Juan.)
   ii. *Le sacaron la muela del juicio a Juan.* (*Sacaron la muela del juicio a Juan.)
   iii. *Le examinaron los dientes al caballo.* (*Examinaron los dientes al caballo.)
   iv. *Le rompieron la pata a la mesa.* (*Rompieron la pata a la mesa.)
   v.   *Le lavaron las manos a Luis.* (*Lavaron las manos a Luis.)
11 It appears that many scholars who claim that IO pronoun doubling is mandatory are from Argentina (Belloro 2007, 2015; MC Cuervo 2003: 34; Colantoni 2002; Masullo 1982: 60; etc.). A few Chilean linguists can be added to that list (Silva-Corvalán and Hurtado, the latter not quoted in this book). All of them are close to the region where DO doubling for animates (in postverbal position) is also common. It also appears that most scholars who insist on the optionality of pronoun doubling with postverbal IOs are from Spain. The data show that an IO without a duplicating pronoun is more frequent in Spain than in Latin America. See, among others, Belloro (2007: 141), Company Company (2006: 539), García-Miguel (1995), Vázquez Rozas (2006: 84). One factor affecting the counts might be postverbal **verbeds** that are duplicated with *le/les*: <u>los datos</u> *les sorprendieron* **a las investigadoras de la UNAM**. A count distinguishing those false <u>verbees</u> is an issue for further research.
12 I changed **bold** in Weissenrieder (1995) to double underline to indicate the <u>IO</u>.
13 When the <u>verber</u> is inanimate and the **verbed** is animate, many languages mark the **verbed** as if it were a <u>verbee</u>. Those verbs are a subset of the PSYCH(OLOGICAL) VERBS. Roughly speaking, psych verbs express cognition, emotion, or perception, and the more interesting psych verbs are those whose **verbed** is animate and whose <u>verber</u> is inanimate. *Fear* and *frighten* are the two prototypical types of psych verbs. Interestingly, if the <u>verber</u> of *astonish* is inanimate, *astonish* would be a *frighten* verb; if both <u>verber</u> and **verbed** are inanimate, *astonish* would be a *fear* verb. The research on psych verbs is extensive. Psych transitive verbs tend to mark their **verbed** as if it were a <u>verbee,</u> in Spanish and in many other languages.
14 Roughly speaking, a participant is MARKED in Spanish as an accusative (as a DO) if it is replaced (or "doubled") with *la/las* or *lo/los*. It is marked with the dative case (as an IO) if it can be replaced or "doubled" with *le/les*. The other pronouns (*me, te, nos, os*) do not differentiate a DO from an IO. Interestingly, it is almost never a problem!
15 The marker is, of course, not necessarily *a*. But it is a preposition-like marker that indicates a *locus* (locative/location) in the corresponding language. The dative is deep down the final location of the gift. "The term dative is related to Latin *dare* 'to give' and is meant to reflect a participant who is a recipient, either of an object or of a more abstract entity", as Butt (2006: 14) explains the origin of the dative case; that is, the case of the IO.
16 This might be a rule of many languages. A rule of atypical (non-default) word order.
17 Similar sentences are common in Ecuador (Suñer & Yepes 1988). A reviewer observed that the same phenomenon is present in several bilingual areas in the Hispanic world (Paraguay, the Basque Country, among others). I thank the reviewer for that clarification.
18 Translations from Gutiérrez Ordóñez and RAE by this author.
19 Although *interesar* is overwhelmingly expressed with subject and "IO", there is evidence that *interesar* is transitive; that is, *interesar* has <u>verber</u> and **verbed**.

   (i) *Los asuntos de familia no interesan a los republicanos* (*El País*, Spain, Dec. 23, 2020).
   'Family issues do not interest Republicans'.

Los republicanos no se interesan en los asuntos de familia; los republicanos no están interesados en los asuntos de familia. (cf. *los republicanos no se importan en/por los asuntos de familia; *los republicanos no están importados en/por los asuntos de familia).

Gutiérrez Ordóñez (1999: 1879–1880) offers these examples:

(i) *Rosa la interesó en el arte.* (His Ex. 68b)
(ii) *El arte interesa a los alumnos.* (His Ex. 70a)
(ii) *Unos alumnos interesados por el arte.* (His Ex. 70b)

20 The tests for the distinction between argumental and non-argumental IOs in Gutiérrez Ordóñez (1999: 1882–1890) are not as conclusive as desired, as he himself recognizes, "En resumen, las dos primeras pruebas muestran [aunque no de forma inequívoca] que poseen un comportamiento semejante al de los dativos valenciales". ("To summarize, the first two tests show [albeit not unequivocally] that they behave like argumental datives". Translation by this author).

21 The DO and the IO are called in traditional Spanish grammar the COMPLEMENTO *directo* and the COMPLEMENTO *indirecto*.

22 Marcos Marín makes the point referring to the DO only. *Fusíleme también*, pero no **fusile a mí también*. More than new information, *a mí* here shows change in reference. That is, if you are going to shoot someone else, shoot me as well.

23 Similar sentences are common in Ecuador (Suñer & Yepes 1988). A reviewer observed that the same phenomenon is present in several bilingual areas in the Hispanic world (Paraguay, the Basque Country; among others). I thank the reviewer for that clarification.

24 (i) a. *Se me acercó.* (655. Normalized frequency = 1.88 cases per million. Corpes XXI, July 2021).

(ii) *Se me acercó a mí.* (0 results).
(iii) *Se acercó a mí.* (417. Normalized frequency = 1.2 cases per million. Corpes XXI, July 2022). 417 is 38.9% of 1072 (655 + 417).

25 *Le/les* becomes *se* before a pronoun beginning with /l/-. Thus, **le la dieron* becomes *se la dieron.*

26 As observed in González (2021: 57–58), there is at least one sentence in English that requires a DO and an IO:

(i) This jerk gave me **the finger**.
(ii) #This jerk gave me.
(iii) #This jerk gave the finger.

If (i) is true, (ii) is not true (without *the finger*). Sentence (iii) will only be true if this person has just one finger, and he gave it to someone. For a transplant, for example. This is an unlikely state of affairs.

27 If one wanted to explain the "doubling" with these two sentences, *a su madre* would be accounted for with a putative rule of doubling when expressing inalienable possession (Jaeggli 1980: 62), as shown in §4.2 and below in §4.4.3. The "doubling" with *a los asuntos* would be a tough assignment to explain. With the rule in (10), these two sentences have the pronoun and the verbee because the latter is new information. As for (27c), observe these sentences as a first utterance in an exchange or as an answer to a question about Felipe. They are ordered, in the opinion of this author, from more to less FELICITOUS. A sentence is FELICITOUS if it is "well-suited for the purpose" (Nordquist 2019, paraphrasing Mark Liberman).

(i) A Felipe le duele **un pie**. (One of Felipe's feet is hurting.)
(ii) Le duele **un pie**.
(iii) Le duele **un pie** a Felipe.

28 Glosses by Belloro were slightly altered to make them consistent with the glosses throughout the book.
29 The argumental vs. non-argumental distinction was proposed by Strozer (1976).
30 I read part of his work around 1990. Wake Forest University's library does not have a copy of this book. Therefore, I could not confirm this quote.
31 www.actfl.org/sites/default/files/reports/Assigning_CEFR_Ratings_To_ACTFL_Assessments.pdf
32 As a teacher and syntactician who has researched the IO for 30 years, I still find it difficult to follow Gutiérrez Ordóñez (1999: 1882–1890) tests for the argumenthood or non argumentality of IOs. There is no doubt that it would be frustrating for teachers or advanced L2 learners of Spanish to follow his discussion. However, understanding the meaning contribution of a verbee in a sentence is a much easier task, as Chapter 3 shows.

References

Aissen, Judith. 2003. Differential object marking: Iconicity vs. economy. *Natural Language and Linguistic Theory* 21. 435–483. www.jstor.org/stable/4048040

Alsina, Alex. 1993. *Predicate composition: A theory of syntactic function alternations*. Stanford, CA: Stanford University. (Doctoral dissertation). https://www.researchgate.net/publication/351617884_Predicate_composition_A_theory_of_syntactic_function_alternations/link/60a13c0d458515c265991c73/download

Aranovich, Roberto. 2011. *Optional agreement and grammatical functions: A corpus study of dative clitic doubling in Spanish*. Pittsburgh: University of Pittsburgh. (Doctoral dissertation). http://d-scholarship.pitt.edu/6209/4/Optional_agreement_and_grammatical_functions.pdf

Barrenechea, Ana María & Orecchia, Teresa. 1970–1971. La duplicación de objetos directos e indirectos en el español hablado en Buenos Aires. *RPhil* 14. 58–83. www.jstor.org/stable/44943055

Bello, Andrés & Cuervo, Rufino José. [1847]1941. *Gramática de la lengua castellana*. Buenos Aires: Librería Perlado.

Belloro, Valeria. 2007. *Spanish clitic doubling: A study of the syntax-pragmatics interface*. Buffalo, NY: State University of New York at Buffalo. (Doctoral dissertation). https://rrg.caset.buffalo.edu/rrg/Belloro-Spanish_Clitic_Doubling.pdf

Belloro, Valeria. 2015. *To the right of the verb: An investigation of clitic doubling and right dislocation in three Spanish dialects*. Cambridge, UK: Cambridge Scholars Publishing. www.cambridgescholars.com/resources/pdfs/978-1-4438-8039-8-sample.pdf

Bossong, Georg. 1991. Differential object marking in romance and beyond. In Wanner, Dieter & Kibbee, Douglas A. (eds.), *New analyses in Romance linguistics*, 143–170. Amsterdam/Philadelphia: Benjamins. https://benjamins.com/catalog/cilt.69

Bossong, Georg. 2021. DOM and linguistic typology: A personal view. In Kabatek, Johannes & Obrist, Philipp & Wall, Albert (eds.), *Differential object marking in Romance: The third wave*, 21–36. Berlin/Boston: De Gruyter. https://doi.org/10.1515/9783110716207

Butt, Miriam. 2006. *Theories of case*. New York: Cambridge University Press. https://doi.org/10.1017/CBO9781139164696

Colantoni, Laura. 2002. Clitic doubling, null objects and clitic climbing in the Spanish of Corrientes. In Gutiérrez Rexac, Javier (ed.), *From words to discourse: Trends* in *Spanish semantics and pragmatics*, 321–336. Amsterdam: Elsevier. https://doi.org/10.1163/9780585475295_018

Company Company, Concepción. 2006. El objeto indirecto. In Company Company, Concepción (ed.), *Sintaxis histórica de la lengua española. Primera parte: La frase verbal*, 479–574. Ciudad de México: Universidad Nacional Autónoma de México/Fondo de Cultura Económica. www.fondodeculturaeconomica.com/Ficha/9786071620415/F

Correas, Gonzalo. [1626]1954. *Arte de la lengua española castellana*. Edition and preface by Emilio Alarcos García. Madrid: Consejo Superior de Investigaciones Científicas. *Revista de Filología Española*. Anejo LVI.

Cuervo, María Cristina. 2003. *Datives at large*. Cambridge, MA: MIT. (Doctoral dissertation), www.ai.mit.edu/projects/dm/theses/cuervo03.pdf

Cuervo, Rufino José. [1847]1941. Notas a la gramática de la lengua castellana de D. Andrés Bello. In Bello, Andrés & Cuervo, Rufino José (eds.), *Gramática de la lengua castellana*. Buenos Aires: Librería Perlado.

Davis, Anthony R. 2001. *Linking by types in the hierarchical lexicon*. Standfor, CA: CSLI/The University of Chicago Press. https://press.uchicago.edu/ucp/books/book/distributed/L/bo3633032.html

Demonte, Violeta. 1995. Dative alternation in Spanish. *Probus* 7(1). 5–30. https://doi.org/10.1515/prbs.1995.7.1.5

Fábregas, Antonio. 2013. Differential object marking in Spanish: State of the art. *Borealis: An International Journal of Spanish Linguistics* 1–80. https://doi.org/10.7557/1.2.2.2603

García, Erica C. 1975. *The role of theory in linguistic analysis: The Spanish pronoun system*. Amsterdam: North-Holland.

Gómez Torrego, Leonardo. 1999. *Gramática didáctica del español*. 5ª ed. Madrid: Ediciones SM. www.casadellibro.com/libro-gramatica-didactica-del-espanol/9788467541359/1855028

González, Luis H. 1997. Transitivity and structural case marking in psych verbs. *A fragment of an HPSG grammar of Spanish*. Davis, CA: University of California. (Doctoral Dissertation). https://www.proquest.com/openview/4bba6135fcdbc9c5749d75bed674d68a/1?pq-origsite=gscholar&cbl=18750&diss=y

González, Luis H. 2021. *The fundamentally simple logic of language: Learning a second language with the tools of the native speaker*. London: Routledge. www.routledge.com/9780367688318

González, Luis H. 2022. *Understanding and teaching reflexive sentences in Spanish*. London: Routledge. https://www.routledge.com/9781032101873

Goyteortúa, Jesús. 1949. *Lluvia roja*. N. York (cit. ind.).

Gutiérrez Ordóñez, Salvador. 1999. Los dativos. In Bosque Muñoz, Ignacio & Demonte Barreto, Violeta (eds.), *Gramática descriptiva de la lengua española*, Vol. 2, 1855–1930. Madrid: Espasa Calpe. www.rae.es/obras-academicas/obras-linguisticas/gramatica-descriptiva-de-la-lengua-espanola

Jaeggli, Osvaldo. 1980. *On some phonologically-null elements in syntax*. Cambridge, MA: MIT. (Doctoral dissertation). http://hdl.handle.net/1721.1/15852

Jaeggli, Osvaldo. 1982. *Topics in Romance syntax*. Foris: Dordrecht.

Kayne, Richard. 1975. *French syntax: The transformational cycle*. Cambridge, MA: MIT Press. https://mitpress.mit.edu/9780262612173/french-syntax/

Keniston, Hayward. 1937. *The syntax of Castilian prose: The sixteenth century*. Chicago: The University of Chicago Press. http://onlinebooks.library.upenn.edu/webbin/book/lookupid?key=ha000908129

Laca, Brenda. 2006. El objeto directo. La marcación preposicional. In Company Company, Concepción (ed.), *Sintaxis histórica de la lengua española. Primera parte. La frase verbal*, 423–475. México, DF: Universidad Nacional Autónoma de México/Fondo de Cultura Económica. www.fondodeculturaeconomica.com/Ficha/9786071620415/F

Lenz, Rodolfo. 1925. La oración y sus partes. *Estudios de gramática general y castellana*. 2a ed. Madrid: Revista de Filología Española.

Levin, Beth & Rappaport Hovav, Malka. 2006. *Argument realization*. Cambridge: Cambridge University Press. https://doi.org/10.1017/CBO9780511610479

Marcos Marín, Francisco. 1978. *Estudios sobre el pronombre*. Madrid: Gredos. (PDF) Estudios sobre el pronombre | Francisco Marcos-Marín-Academia.edu

Maldonado, Ricardo. [1999]2006. *A media voz. Problemas conceptuales del clítico se*. México, DF: Universidad Nacional Autónoma de México. www.iifilologicas.unam.mx/chiifl 9/doku.php/a_media_voz

Masullo, Pascual J. 1992. *Incorporation and case theory in Spanish: A crosslinguistic perspective*. Seattle, WA: University of Washington. (Doctoral dissertation). www.scribd.com/document/409657865/1992-Masullo-Incorporation-and-case-theory-in-Spanish-pdf#

Nordquist, Richard. 2019. Felicity conditions: Definition and examples. *ThoughtCo*. www.thoughtco.com/felicity-conditions-speech-1690855 (Last accessed 2023).

Poston, Lawrence, Jr. 1953. The redundant object pronoun in contemporary Spanish. *Hispania* 36. 263–272. www.jstor.org/stable/335092

RAE/ASALE (Real Academia Española y Asociación de Academias de la Lengua Española). 2009. *Nueva gramática de la lengua española. Sintaxis II*. Madrid: Espasa. www.rae.es/obras-academicas/gramatica/nueva-gramatica-morfologia-y-sintaxis

RAE/ASALE (Real Academia Española y Asociación de Academias de la Lengua Española). 2010. *Nueva gramática de la lengua española. Manual*. Bogotá: Editorial Planeta Colombiana. S.A. www.rae.es/obras-academicas/gramatica/manual-de-la-nueva-gramatica

Strozer, Judith. 1976. *Clitics in Spanish*. Los Ángeles, CA: University of California. (Doctoral dissertation). www.worldcat.org/title/clitics-in-spanish/oclc/3145731

Suñer, Margarita. 1982. *Syntax and semantics of Spanish presentational sentence types*. Washington, DC: Georgetown University Press. ISBN-10: 0878400842

Suñer, Margarita & Yepes, María. 1988. Null definite objects in Quiteño. *Linguistic Inquiry* 19(3). 511–519. www.jstor.org/stable/25164909

Vázquez Rozas, Victoria. 2006. Gustar-type verbs. In Clements, Joseph Clancy & Yoon, Jiyoung (eds.), *Functional approaches to Spanish syntax*, 80–114. New York: Palgrave Macmillan. https://pdfs.semanticscholar.org/49d3/117788a84917f086ae694f6ae482ff075fce.pdf?_ga=2.201348755.369220713.1597701565-1866771009.1594303638

Weissenrieder, Maureen. 1995. Indirect object doubling: Saying things twice in Spanish. *Hispania* 1. 169–177. https://doi.org/10.2307/345242

Index

accomplishment 39, 44, 61n3
accusative 10–12, 15, 16, 25, 32n4, 45, 48, 57, 61, 62n22, 73, 74, 105n14
achievement 39, 61n3
activity **38**, 39, 44
applicative 33
argumental 50, 52, 81, 87–89, 91–94, 106n20, 107n29
argument structure 66–67, 80, 87, 104n5
atypical (marked word order) 78–79, 83, 90, 105n16

Belloro, Valeria 14, 32, 33n22, 61n11, 66–68, 71–72, 84, 88, 91, 93, 104n6
belongee 8, 32, 45
benefactee 4, 8, 16, **17**, 21, 24, 32n4, 33n13, 37, 40, 42, 45–46, 48, 52, 60, 61n6, 73, 80, 82, 89
beneficiary 4

clitic doubling 65–67, 89, 91, 104n2
Company Company, Concepción 32n5, 41, 66–67, 72, 88, 91–92, 105n11
Cuervo, María Cristina (MC Cuervo) 5, 33, 37–39, 41, 43, 45–46, 52, 58, 60, 60n2, 67, 105n11
Cuervo, Rufino José (RJ Cuervo) 12, 14–15, 18, 74

dative 5, 7, 12–16, 23, 25, 30, 32n8, 33, 37, 38, 39, 41, 45–46, 48
dative marking 72
dative overriding 11–12
differential object marking (DOM) 74–75
doubling *see* clitic doubling

Dowty, David 7
duplicated 8, **17**, 31n2, 37, 42, 67, 78, 84, 104n11

entailment 1–2, 5, 9–12, 16, **17**, 19–20, 24–25, 46, 48, 52, 58, 62n22, 62n25
experiencer 5, 17, **38**, 41, 45, **55**, 60, 91

Fábregas, Antonio 12, 74, 84
Fernández-Ordóñez, Inés 13–14, 32n10
Fernández Ramírez, Salvador 13–15

goal 5, 17, 41, 45, 60, 75
Gutiérrez Ordóñez, Salvador 19, 32, 66–68, 73–74, 78–79, 81–82, 84, 87, 89, 91–92, 105n18, 106n19, 106n20, 107n32

happenee 12, 32
heaviness (heavier) 39, 41

inchoative 38
indirect object drop/IO drop 65, 68–69, 72, 76, 78, 87, 94, 104n8
inference 8–9, 104n6
intransitive 2, 3, 15, **38**, 43, **49**, **50**, 92
intransitively 92
intransitivization/intransitivizing 7n6, 11, 19, 21, 41, 77

Jaeggli, Osvaldo 65, 67, 69, 91, 105n10, 106n27

known information (48 entries)

Lapesa, Rafael 13, 14, 25, 33n18
leísmo (dialectal *leísmo*) 11–15, 30, 33n21, 46, 74, 78

Index   111

leísmo (general *leísmo*) 11–12, 14–15, 33n21, 46, 74, 78
Levin, Beth 15–16
lexical entry 50, 67, 75, 77, 104n5

malefactee 4, 8, 16, 24, **27**, 32n4, 33, 37, 40, 45, 46, 48, 52, 60, 61n6, 80, 89
maleficiary 4
Marcos Marín, Francisco 13–14, 25, 32n5, 65, 68, 84
marked 11, 16, 20, 22, 32n7, 32n8, 40, 42, 46, 48, **49**, 56, 62n22, 62n25, 75, 79, 83, 89, 90, 105n14

nominalization 24–25
nominative 25, 32n4, 57, 62n22
non argumental 66, 77, 81, 91–92

passivize 12, 48
possessor 5, **38**, 45, **51**, 60
primary (object) 4, **17**, 21, 33n13, 40, 46, 61n6
productive 4, 18
psychological verb 13, 15–16, **38**, **50**
Pylkkänen, Liina 33n15

RAE/ASALE (2009) 9, 11, 20, 24–25, 32n5, 66, 86, 92
RAE/ASALE (2010) 5, 13–14, 16, 60, 67, 76, 83–84, 86–89, 92
recipient 3, 5, 17, **38**, 40–41, 45, **55**, 60, 80, 105n15

redundant 65
referent 4, 13, 15, 28, 30, 40
resultative **10**, 11, 19–20, 74, 79

secondary (object) 4, 21, 33n13, 40, 61
semantic role 5, 17, 33n15, 39, 41, 45–46, 58, 60
source **38**, 41, 45, 60
Suñer, Margarita 67, 84, 99n4, 105n17, 196n23

topic 77, 86
topicalization 19, 45, 57, 76–77, 79, 85; verbed topicalization 11, 77; <u>verbee</u> topicalization 77, 79, 86–88
topicalized 8, 11–12, 15, **17**, 19, 24–25, 31n2, 37, 77–78, 86–89
transitive 2, 3, 8, 32n11, **38**, 43, **49**, **55**, 56, 60, 105n13

unaccusative 3, 11, 32n4, 38, 62n20, 80
underlying 2, 25, 28, 76, 78, 87

Vázquez Rozas 15, 19, 23, 71–72, 88, 105n11
verberless 3, 8, 11, 16, 19, 23–24, 28, 32n4, 33n14, 43, 45, 48, 52, 59, 60, 61n13, 80, 89
VVASP (<u>verber</u>/verbed argument selection principle) 2

world knowledge 6, 66, 68, 75, 83–84, 86

For Product Safety Concerns and Information please contact our EU representative GPSR@taylorandfrancis.com
Taylor & Francis Verlag GmbH, Kaufingerstraße 24, 80331 München, Germany

www.ingramcontent.com/pod-product-compliance
Lightning Source LLC
Chambersburg PA
CBHW051754230426
43670CB00012B/2289